# What's Your Status?

LeeAnne Locken

© 2012 by LeeAnne Locken
All rights reserved. Except as permitted under the U.S. Copyright Act of 1976, no part of this publication may be reproduced, distributed or transmitted in any form or by any means, or stored in a database or retrieval system, without the prior written permission of the publisher.

# Contents

Introduction .......................... 4
January ................................. 5
February ............................. 37
March ................................. 66
April .................................. 98
May ................................. 129
June ................................. 161
July ................................. 192
August ............................. 224
September ........................ 256
October ............................ 287
November ........................ 319
December ........................ 350

# Introduction

"It's Just Facebook!" ...or at least that is what my boyfriend would say to me every morning when I began this journey. He couldn't understand why it was so important to me to dedicate my time every morning to the computer. He couldn't see that it wasn't the machine... it was the audience. And it was my friends on Facebook who chatted with me every morning that made me want to keep it up!

I started this collection of positive posts about three years ago -- just before my grandmother passed away. Her mission in life was always to help others and I grew up with that as my example of how to live, so it became a logical and comfortable direction to take my life. I wasn't sure if the posts would mean anything to anyone but me, but I took a leap of faith. And three years later, I sit here writing a book about it... a collection of morning posts meant to INSPIRE, MOTIVATE, ENCOURAGE and EMPOWER others to THINK, ACT, BELIEVE... and to SHINE!

# January

## January 1

Remember to be GRATEFUL for everything in your life that has brought you this far and EXCITED to see what new and positive things lay ahead this year!! This is a year to let go of all that has held you back and listen for the direction of where God wants you to go!!!
HAPPY NEW YEAR, EVERYONE!!

## January 2

Today is the first day of the
rest of your life…
What will you do with it?
How will you live it?
Ask yourself these simple
questions, then GO GET IT!!
You are a one-of-a-kind
masterpiece of GOD!
Now go LIVE like it!!

## January 3

Get ready to make room for what
God wants in your life!!
Sometimes we have to let go
of what isn't working
so he can show us what will!
Remember ~ God closes doors
no one can open and
opens doors no one can close!!
Hope everyone has a
Magical Monday!!
Now, coffee please!! =)

## January 4

I believe that
we cannot change yesterday, and
we cannot predict tomorrow, but
we can live today!!
SO BE ALIVE!!!
Never let one day pass by
without a smile!
Who's ready for a
TERRIFIC DAY?
ME! ME! ME!
Now where's the coffee? :)

## January 5

I believe we should all
take a good look at
what we are focusing on
each day… it guides our direction,
our opinions, and our attitudes!
Today ~ try to only focus on the
good!! Watch how happy and
content your day gets!
An 'attitude of gladitude'
leads to a very
Happy & Healthy life!!

## January 6

I believe your past makes you,
but it shouldn't keep you!
Your future waits to greet you,
but it shouldn't control you!!
LIVE FOR TODAY
or you will miss what you never
knew you had!!
Breathe in each moment!!
They are ALL precious and should
ALL be TREASURED!!

# January 7

Today I am repeating to myself ~ "Lord grant me the STRENGTH to be content where I am, the PATIENCE to wait on YOUR TIMING, and the FAITH to remember that you have your hand always on my heart!!"
Have a blessed day, Y'all!!

## January 8

Believe that to realize the worth
of an anchor,
you must go through the storm!
So don't fear the tough times ~
stand strong!!
When those storms end,
YOU will be stronger, wiser and
more prepared for the next one!
Very few lessons in life are easy,
but they are always worth it
if we learn something!!
Good Morning, Y'all!!

## January 9

I believe that everything in life
happens for a reason!
God causes certain doors to close
to you in order to
move you in the right direction!!
Nothing happens TO us ~
it all happens FOR us!!
When you view life this way…
every day becomes exciting!!

## January 10

I believe that when our
passion and purpose
are greater than our
fear and worry,
we are able to accomplish
great things!!
Two things drive humans…
desire for success and
fear of failure!
Which one are you set on –
the carrot or the rod?
Dream big ~ and stay focused on
SUCCESS!!

## January 11

I truly believe it takes COURAGE
to stand out…
but nothing to fit in!!
Be who you are.
Your life is yours and
determined by the Lord,
NOT anyone else!!
You are an amazing,
one-of-a-kind creation meant to
SHINE!!

## January 12

When life gives you a rainy day,
you should play in the puddles!!!
Complaining and whining
won't bring you back the
sunshine! When you learn to love
and accept where you are,
then God will give you more!!
Today, have an attitude of
gratitude!!

# January 13

Wake up this morning singing...
'Forget your troubles,
come on get HAPPY!!!'
Hand all your worries and
problems to GOD and then, with a
positive attitude,
GO MAKE IT A GREAT DAY!!!
Life can only affect you if YOU
let it!! YOU are in control!!
It's YOUR life!! Get it?
It's ALL UP TO... YOU!!!

## January 14

When we can love without fear,
trust without question,
need without demand,
want without restriction, and
desire without inhibition…
then we will be at peace with
ourselves and our world!!

# January 15

My Grandma used to remind me to ALWAYS treat others the way I wanted to be treated!!!
They may forget what you said, but they will ALWAYS remember how you made them feel!!!
And how YOU made them feel is how THEY will feel about YOU!!
Go make someone HAPPY today!!

## January 16

God wants us to
GIVE without expectation,
ACCEPT without reservation, and
LOVE with hesitation!!
When you can do this ~
You are truly LIVING the life
God wants for you!!

# January 17

Sing it with me ~
"Happy, Happy, Joy, Joy!!"
The more we sing celebrations, the
more we bring them to pass!
"Forget your troubles ~
COME ON GET HAPPY!!"
Proven technique: behave the way
you want to feel and then,
soon enough
YOU WILL!!

## January 18

Everyone should remember to
PAY IT FORWARD!!!
Make someone's day!!
Do a random act of kindness,
you'll find it goes a long way!!
After all,
what goes around comes around!

## January 19

We are motivated
by only two things in life ~
the carrot and the stick!!
The truth is people will do more
to avoid pain than to gain reward!
Now is the time to change that!!
Make your life
MORE rewarding!!
It's all up to you!!!

## January 20

I believe that until you realize
YOU are the creator
of your own misery,
you will never be truly happy…
for it is how you react to any given
situation that brings you
happiness!!
Change the way you SEE things
and the things you see will
change!!
Here's to a
THOUGHTFUL DAY!!

## January 21

Now get to SINGING!!
When you know yourself
then you are empowered, but
when you accept yourself…
you become invincible!!!
Happy Martin Luther King Day,
Everyone!!
We are all created equal and
should be treated as such!!!

# January 22

Sometimes we just need
someone to show us something
we can't see for ourselves…
and then we are changed forever!!
Do something nice, something
sweet and something daring FOR
someone else today,
and believe me ~
it will change YOU!!
Spread the LOVE!!

## January 23

I strongly believe that FEAR
should never decide LOVE!!!
Choose love
for the positive reasons
and never the negative ones!!
Have a Happy Day,
Everyone!!

**January 24**

Our lives improve ONLY
when we take chances ~
and the first and most difficult
risk we can take is
to be honest with ourselves!!
Honesty is one of the highest
forms of respect!!

# January 25

God wants us to wear our blessings with pride and joy!! Don't let others' jealousy keep you from singing God's praises of how blessed you are!! No one knows all have been through but God, and He rewards us for living the right way!! It's not "look how great I am" ~ it's "LOOK HOW GREAT GOD HAS BEEN TO ME!!"

## January 26

I wonder… has the world gotten so that we would rather be lied to and made happy than told the truth so the problem can be fixed?
Think about it.
People of character do the right thing, not because they think it will change the world, but because they REFUSE
to be changed by the world!!
HONESTY and TRUTH takes COURAGE, even if it stirs another, it's still the best choice!
Liars are cowards!
CHOOSE to be HONEST today!

## January 27

No matter where you come from
or who raised you
or how bad your life has been,
YOU make your life what it is,
and blame is a dead end!!
Decide what and who you want in
your life and then find a way to
MAKE IT HAPPEN!!

## January 28

It doesn't matter who you were
a decade ago, a year ago,
or even yesterday...
what matters is
who you are TODAY
and who you want to be
tomorrow!
Let go of the past…
it will only anchor you
to your problems!
Forgive yourself
so that others can too!
And most of all,
LOVE YOURSELF!!!

## January 29

No matter how bad life is
treating you right now,
there is always someone
who is worse off than you!
Don't surround yourself with
sorrow! Life can be hard!
Life can be fun! Life can be kind,
and life can be mean!
Have the right attitude and life can
be whatever YOU want it to be!
Now for some COFFEE and
LAUGHTER!!
MAKE IT A HAPPY DAY!!

## January 30

There are moments in your life
that make you
and set the course
of who you are going to be!
Sometimes they are little, subtle
moments. Sometimes, they are big
ones you never saw coming.
No one asks for their life to
change, but it does!!
It's what you do after that counts!!
That's when you find out
who you are...

## January 31

I know that FAITH
is daring the heart to go beyond
what the eyes can see and
the mind can understand!!!
DREAM your dream,
BELIEVE in yourself, and
LIVE your life to its fullest!!

# February

# February 1

Woke up to a WHITE WINTER WONDERLAND!!
It's just beautiful (from inside my house near the fire)!
Remember, for every beauty, there's an eye somewhere to see it.
For every truth, there's an ear somewhere to hear it.
And for every love, there's a heart somewhere to receive it!
Hope everyone is warm and safe!!

## February 2

Life isn't about being who
everyone else wants you to be...
it's about being yourself and
finding someone who loves
every bit of it!!!
God created a perfect work of art
with each of us ~
SHINE in your beauty!!

## February 3

One day you will see that
it has finally all come together!
That day when you look back,
laugh at what has passed,
and ask yourself, "How did I get
through all of that?"
So for today, stay focused on what
is truly important
and have FAITH that
God has a plan!!
Now grab your coffee and let's
"Get R Done!!"

## February 4

Before you complain
about how the world treats you,
you should think of
how you treat the world!!
Remember, great people are those
who make others feel that they,
too, can become great!!!
Make today about someone
else's happiness!!!
Trust me ~
the return is worth it!

## February 5

We should love completely ~
give second chances ~
and don't be afraid to make
mistakes!!
We all do!!
Just learn from them,
try not to repeat them,
and move on!!
Without taking chances,
you are simply standing still!!
I'm off to work!

## February 6

The Light of God surrounds You,
The Love of God enfolds You,
The Power of God protects You,
and the Presence of God
watches over You!
Wherever You are, God Is!
Hope EVERYONE has a
BLESSED DAY!!

## February 7

Welcome a new day
with a smile on your lips,
love in your heart,
good thoughts in your mind, and
you'll always have a
WONDERFUL one!!!!
It's a Magical day, Y'all ~
Go make it HAPPEN!

## February 8

I love wifi on the plane!
It's going to make the
two hour-forty minute flight
much better!!
Today is a great day to
make someone else happy
just because you can!!
Hope Y'all are having a
TERRIFIC DAY!!!

## February 9

If you are looking for motivation, sometimes the biggest source of inspiration comes from the person you see in the mirror everyday!! Look yourself in the face and say out loud,
"I CAN DO ANYTHING!!"
Now go make it
a FABULOUS day!

## February 10

I'm sharing my recipe
for happiness:
Live with enthusiasm,
smile for no reason,
love without conditions,
act with purpose,
listen with your heart, and
laugh often!!!
Hope everyone has
a Thrilling day!

## February 11

I saw this today and thought…
now that's the TRUTH!!!
"I am not as good as I should be,
I am not as good as I could be,
but THANK GOD,
I am better than I used to be!"
Every day, choose to get better
and better!!

## February 12

If you can imagine it,
you can achieve it… and
if you can dream it,
you can become it.
Hope and Faith pave the path
that leads us to our goals!!
With determination in your heart
and a smile on your face ~
YOU CAN DO IT!!
Have a SUPER DAY
EVERYONE!!

**February 13**

I believe God gives us all
a purpose in life…
it's our choice what we do with it.
So choose wisely,
speak out for what is right,
and stop the ignorance.
Make 2013 better!
My motivation is sponsored
by the Word of God.
It's a great way to start the day!!
Have a Blessed day, Y'all!!

## February 14

I want to wish EVERYONE ~
♥ Happy Valentine's Day!!!
Today, I want to say
THANK YOU to you all
for being my friends
and let you know how much
I treasure each message and
thought posted!!
You have made me smile,
laugh and cry with happiness!!
YOU are ALL GREATLY
APPRECIATED!!

## February 15


I believe God puts obstacles
in your way
so that YOU can discover
the magnitude of the strength
you possess!!
Don't look at obstacles as
problems…
Look at them as lessons!!

## February 16

When you treat people as they are,
they will remain as they are,
BUT, when you treat them as they
could be… they can become
what they should be!!!
Today, help someone
rise to their BEST!!!
Today, help someone
believe in themselves!!

## February 17

What lies behind you, and what lies in front of you pales in comparison to what lies inside of you!!! Today, look in the mirror and tell yourself, "OH YES I CAN!!!" Go make it an amazing day, Y'all!!

## February 18

With courage,
you will dare to take risks…
have the strength to be
compassionate…
and the wisdom to be humble!!
Courage is the foundation
of integrity!
Make it a day filled with
COURAGE!!

## February 19

I believe…
that every one of us alone
has the power to direct the course
of our lives by choosing what
actions we will or will not take!
You always have a choice!!
What will you choose to do today?
Make it beautiful!!

## February 20

Don't forget… Jesus said,
"I am the light of the world.
If you follow me, you won't have
to walk in darkness,
because you will have the light
that leads to life."
~John 8:12...
Have a blessed day everyone!!

## February 21

I believe that morning is
God's way of saying,
"Live life one more time,
make a difference, touch a heart,
encourage a mind and
inspire a soul!"
So… what are you waiting for??
Get up and DO IT!!
Make it a MAGICAL DAY!!!

## February 22

We should challenge
the impossible,
explore beyond our comfort zone,
refuse to be limited by boundaries,
and never settle for less
than we deserve!!
And since you are a child of God,
YOU DESERVE THE BEST!!
Make it an amazing day!!

## February 23

I believe…
that good things come
to those who wait,
but GREAT things come
to those that get out there and
MAKE IT HAPPEN!!!
I hope everyone is having a
Wonderful day!!

## February 24

Try singing...
"Good Morning, World!!"
Just want to let you know that
no matter what you send my way
today, I WILL have a
GREAT DAY!!!!
Now let's grab a cup coffee and
ALL keep singing!!

**February 25**

Do you ever think,
"What can I do to help
someone else?"
I ask you today to do that!!
The less we are consumed
with SELF,
the happier we will be!!
Helping someone else is a gift
that you have the power to give
every second!!
DO IT TODAY!!

## February 26

We should stand up
for what we believe in!!
We cannot make everyone like us,
but if we remain AUTHENTIC ~
we will be able to like ourselves!!
Be proud of who
God made YOU to be!!
Have a super day, Ya'll,
and pass the coffee!!

## February 27

I am repeating… but
"Those who trust in the Lord
will find new strength!
They will soar high
on wings like eagles."
~Isaiah 40:31
So, for today, catch a breeze and
fly higher than ever enjoying all
that God has created!!
Have a blessed day EVERYONE!!

## February 28

If you want to reach a
state of bliss,
go beyond your ego.
Make a decision to relinquish
the need to control,
the need to be approved, and
the need to judge!
After all, the only one who should
judge is God!

# March

# March 1

All problems
are just illusions of the mind!
What we consider problems
are only situations
that need to be dealt with…
or accepted!!
Look for the positive resolution
and both become
easy to achieve!!
Who's feeling a TERRIFIC DAY
coming on?
WooHoo!!

## March 2

When you are no longer able
to change a situation,
then you are challenged
to change yourself!!
Remember...
woulda, coulda, shoulda... didn't.
If it bothers you, change it.
If you can't change it,
move on and make sure
you get it right next time!
Take today to be YOUR BEST!!

## March 3

I want you to
BELIEVE in yourself
and all that you are…
Know that there is something
inside you that is greater
than any obstacle!!
Remember, challenges
aren't there to stop you...
They are there to see if
YOU have the courage
to defeat them!
Make it a SUCCESSFUL DAY!!

## March 4

A person's OWN HAPPINESS
is not derived from the
SITUATION THEY are IN,
but from the
ATTITUDE THEY HAVE!!!
Remember, an attitude of gratitude
will most definitely lead you to
GLADITUDE!!!

## March 5

Welcome every morning
with a smile!!
Look on the new day
as a special gift,
a golden opportunity to refocus,
reorganize, and recommit!!
Good things come when you let go
of the negative,
so make room for it to be
an awesome day!!

## March 6

Today holds
blessings and miracles
that you don't even know of,
so grab a hold of today with
HOPE and LOVE, and
expect GREAT things to happen!
"Ask, and you shall receive.
Search, and you shall find. Knock,
and the door will be opened
to you."
~Matthew 7:7

## March 7

I'm so happy it is Morning!!
It's a NEW beginning…
a NEW start!!
A chance to reassess and recommit yourself to reaching your goals!! Today you CAN DO ANYTHING!! You just have to do it!! There are only two choices: make progress or make excuses!!
Make it a
MAGICAL DAY!!

## March 8

I BELIEVE…
that when you give your time,
talent and wisdom to helping
others find the key
to THEIR destiny,
YOU will unlock your own!!
Today, have a helpful heart and
enjoy the happiness
it brings you!!

# March 9

I want you to make sure to NEVER let anyone tell you that they are better than you!! You are ONE OF A KIND created by God Almighty… as UNIQUE and SPECIAL as they come!! After all, 'amateurs' built the Ark, but 'professionals' built the Titanic!!! Go SHOW THE WORLD how wonderful you are today!!

## March 10

I know my days are
ALWAYS much better
when I remember to
thank God for what I have
and not focus on what I want!!
When you learn to be TRULY
grateful for where and
who you are in life… that is when
God blesses you
EVEN MORE!!!

# March 11

Morning is God's way of saying,
"GO live life… one more time,
make a difference, touch a heart,
encourage a mind
and inspire a soul!!"
So we ALL better get to it!!
Make it a FANTASTIC DAY!!!
…and pass the coffee!!!

## March 12

I'm sharing the wisdom of my grandmother ~ She used to tell me that worrying is a sin
because it means that I don't have faith that God is in control!
Today, let go of your worries!!
Open your heart to faith!!
Then you will have more room for joy in your life!!

# March 13

When things happen in your life that don't make sense to you, and you don't understand why, it's because God has taken control!! God is a faithful God and will never fail you or let you down!! Let his word give you PROMISE, HOPE and FAITH!!

## March 14

I want you to know that
your day will be even better
if you start it with positivity?
So smile, be happy, be optimistic,
and be positive!
What you put out there
WILL be returned to you!!!
Go and MAKE IT a
MAGICAL DAY!!!

## March 15

Success is waiting
for those who are ready to persist
and face the obstacles in the path
with a positive attitude!!
Remember…
there are only two choices:
make progress or make excuses!!
Which one will you choose?

## March 16

I want YOU to remember to
NEVER hold your head down,
NEVER say 'I can't,'
NEVER limit yourself, and
NEVER stop
believing in yourself!!!
You are special and gifted,
so get up get out and get yours!!!
YOU are PERFECT
in God's eyes, and in mine!

# March 17

It's easy
to turn to God
when we are facing
struggles and hardship,
but it's important to also
turn to him
during the good times!!
Take a long look at
where you are today
and be grateful for your place.
It's right for you, now, and is
preparing you for the adventure
ahead!!! So who's ready for a
THRILLING DAY??
Let's start with COFFEE!!

# March 18

I heard this yesterday
and thought it was too cute
to not pass along to Y'all,
so here goes ~
In order to succeed in life, you
need three things…
a wish bone, a back bone, and
a funny bone!!!
I think I'm covered…
How about YOU?
Make it a FANTASTIC DAY,
EVERYONE!!!
…coffee is ready!!

## March 19

If you create stability,
happiness, and love for yourself,
it won't go away
just because someone else does…
or your circumstances change!!!
So today, practice ~
loving yourself,
believing in yourself, AND
smiling and laughing at yourself!!

# March 20

We should use FAITH
to control US,
not the circumstances
that surround us!!
When you can have peace
in the center of the storm,
then you are showing God
you have FAITH in him!!
"The Lord will fight for you and
you shall hold your peace and
remain at rest"
~Exodus 14:14
Make it Spectacular Day, Y'all!!

## March 21

I love Mondays!!
It's a NEW week,
providing NEW opportunities
and NEW chances
to do GREAT things!!
Whatever your dreams are ~
Don't give up!!
Find a new approach, and
look for the path that is working!!
BELIEVE IN YOURSELF!! ♥
HAPPY DAY, EVERYONE!

# March 22

I was reminded yesterday
that some will only see you
as who you used be, and
some as who you never were
or would be!!
But then,
there are those who will always
see you for who you really are!!
The important thing
to remember is… to
not let the negative affect you ~
hold your head above that and
SMILE, knowing
YOU ARE A UNIQUE WORK
OF ART!!

# March 23

We should never give up
too easily!!
It just takes encouragement,
determination, hard work,
and a positive attitude!
YOU can and WILL succeed
in all that you put my mind to!!!
So look yourself in the mirror and
say ~ "TODAY I WILL BE
SUCCESSFUL & HAPPY!!!"
Make it a Wonderful day!!

## March 24

If you want to reach
a state of bliss,
you must go BEYOND
your ego!!
Make a decision to relinquish
the need to control,
the need to be approved,
and the need to judge!!
Realize that who you ARE and
what you HAVE are
gifts from GOD!!

## March 25

When you create peace
within your own being,
it radiates out into the world!!
The world then becomes a
more peaceful place,
one person at a time!!
You can find peace
by letting go of fear and worries!!
Keep Faith in your heart!!

## March 26

On this day in 2010,
I lost my hero!
My grandmother raised me, and
taught me the Bible, and
taught me what
UNCONDITIONAL LOVE
really is!!
I miss her… and I am
GRATEFUL for ALL of her
teachings!! My morning posts are
because of her!!
I love you GRANDMA!! ♥
Go call your grandmothers today!!

## March 27

Just when you think
you can't go on,
God is there, and
God's Word provides the grace
and love you need to take on
whatever life has to deal out!
"God… thank you for everything!!
I didn't know how strong I was,
until you showed me!
I didn't know what to do,
until you helped me!!
And I didn't know who I was,
until you loved me!"
Don't forget to thank God today!!

## March 28

Wake up every day and say,
"Go Today!! Exciting & New!!!"
Put a smile on your face, and
tell yourself ~
EVERYTHING is POSSIBLE
TODAY!!!!
Make it a
MAGICAL DAY!!

## March 29

When we choose to forgive,
it opens our hearts
so that we can receive everything
God has in store for us!!
Take a deep breath
and leave the details to God!!
If God is for you,
who can be against you?
Sometimes, having class is
having the ability to walk away
from a bad situation
with a smile on your face and
a forgiveness in your heart.
Let go and free yourself for a
BEAUTIFUL TODAY!!

# March 30

Showing love and compassion
and giving words of
encouragement
can make all the difference
in someone giving up…
or going on!!
SERIOUSLY~
There is power in what you say;
speak carefully!!
Go encourage someone
POSITIVELY TODAY and feel
the same encouragement
rise in you!!
It's contagious!!
LIVE WITH PASSION!! ♥

# March 31

He had no servants,
yet they called Him Master.
He had no degree,
yet they called Him Teacher.
He had no medicines,
yet they called Him Healer.
He had no army,
yet kings feared Him…
He won no military battles,
yet He conquered the world.
He committed no crime,
yet they crucified Him.
He was buried in a tomb,
yet Jesus rose
and lives today...
Happy Easter!! ♥

# April

## April 1

Woke up to April Fool's Day!!!
Hmmm… if you are planning
on playing practical jokes today
(a few people started last night)
PLEASE consider people's
feelings and make them
lighthearted!!
Thank God
for ALL his blessings today!!
HAVE A HAPPY
APRIL FOOL'S DAY!
with COFFEE!!! LOL

# April 2

MLK once said,
"Hatred paralyzes life;
LOVE releases it!
Hatred confuses life;
LOVE harmonizes it.
Hatred darkens life;
LOVE illuminates it!!"
SO remember to FORGIVE
the weaknesses in others,
because GOD forgives
the weaknesses in YOU!!
Holding on to anything negative
will only consume you!!
RELEASE it and
LIVE FREELY!!

# April 3

I smile to show I'm Happy!!!
I cry to show I'm human!!!
I laugh to show I'm alive!!!
I pray to show I'm blessed!!!
But I live…
because it's what GOD wants!

## April 4

If you don't believe
in something greater than yourself,
then you will never achieve
anything greater than yourself!!
Dream BIG!!
It's a new week for a fresh start…
for new opportunities and
new SUCCESS!!!

## April 5

When you do things
the 'right' way
the right things come to you!!
So today, try to inspire someone
in a positive way ~
and feel the wave of inspiration
wash over you in return!

# April 6

These simple measures
will keep you happy...
Before you pray ~ Forgive!!
Before you quit ~ Try!!
Before you retire ~ Save!!
Before you die ~ Give!!
Before you speak ~ Listen!!
Before you write ~ Think!!
Before you spend ~ Earn!!
I find simple logic
works the best!!

# April 7

Confidence doesn't come from
thinking you are perfect…
or flawless!!
That's arrogance!
Confidence comes from
appreciating the beauty
of your texture!
When you have the strength
and courage to allow yourself to
be who you TRULY are,
and not become what others
believe you should be,
then you have found your
confidence!!
Now go and SHINE
like God created you to!!

# April 8

You can choose to be pitiful…
or powerful,
but you can't be both!!
When you pity yourself,
you give the power to others!!
You have the power within you
to do and be whatever you choose,
your ability is unlimited as long as
your belief in yourself is, too!!
Today… choose to be
POWERFUL!!

# April 9

If you spend your time
being jealous of others,
you will NEVER be happy
with yourself. Your daily actions
set the compass for your
attitude and emotions!!
Remember ~ Jealousy is the
mindset of a simplistic mind
whose words are displayed with
animosity… illustrating one's lack
of self-confidence!!
Focus on the joy of your life and
your life WILL BE joyful!!
Have a SMILEY,
"WONKA" DAY!!!

# April 10

True success
is when you reach back
and help bring someone forward
with you!! By helping someone go
further in life, God rewards you
by pushing you further ahead!
You may not end up where you
thought you'd be, but you will
always end up where
you are meant to be . . .
right where God
intended you to be all along!
Become a DREAM RELEASER!!
Help someone
reach their dreams!!!

# April 11

I LOVE THE MORNING!!!
It's newness offers possibilities
we may not even know of!
Don't wait until the conditions
are perfect to begin!
BEGINNING
makes the conditions perfect!!!!
YOU CAN DO IT!!!
Make today the beginning of
something AMAZING!!

# April 12

Words are powerful…
they have the ability to
build you up,
tear you down,
love you and encourage you!!
Be mindful of your words
every second,
especially the ones you use
towards yourself!!!
Just for today ~ try to only use
positive, loving words
and see how happy
your day turns out!!

# April 13

Coffee poured? Check!
Facebook running? Check!
Sunshine? Check!
A day off? Check!
Exactly what is a day off?
laundry, cleaning, dishes...
going to work doesn't sound that bad, after all!! LOL ~
OK, now I'm ready for a wonderful day!
Happy WONDERFUL DAY, Y'ALL!!

# April 14

Each and every day,
we are afforded the opportunity
to make another feel better,
smile, or even laugh.
After all, at the end of the day,
what matters MOST
is not what we have…
but what we have shared!!
We should ALL take that
opportunity today!!

# April 15

I think that for today,
we should surrender our desire
for security
and seek serenity instead!!
When you do, you will look at
your life with new eyes.
May this day bring into your life
something that makes
your face smile
until your eyes light with joy
and your heart sings!!

# April 16

Happiness doesn't mean
everything is perfect!
Perfect is very subjective!!
Happiness is appreciating
what you do have
AND accepting the parts
you cannot change!!
LOVE YOURSELF and OTHERS
as who you/we are…
all UNIQUE works of ART
created by GOD!!

# April 17

For today, let's follow
~Peter 4:8-9…
"Above all,
love each other deeply,
because love covers over
a multitude of sins.
Offer hospitality to one another
without grumbling."
And, I add to that,
be patient and kind
and it WILL be a
beautifully blessed day!!

# April 18

If you want tomorrow to be better,
YOU have to do something
differently today!
Come on!! It's a new week!!
How are YOU going to make it
a GREAT one??
For me, I love the feeling that I get
when I KNOW that something
good is going to happen!
Let's ALL EXPECT IT to be a
GREAT WEEK!!

# April 19

I have come to realize
that when things happen
in your life
that don't make sense to you,
and you don't understand why,
it's because God has taken control.
So when I feel lost, I look at my
GPS ~ God's Placement System,
and though I still may not
know where I am,
I KNOW I'll arrive safely and
exactly when I should!!
FAITH gives me that comfort!!

# April 20

I believe that our life
is deeply affected
by what we FOCUS on!!
When you focus on problems,
you will have more problems!!
When you focus on possibilities,
you will have more opportunities!!
Remember…
an optimist is just someone who,
when finding themself
in hot water…
decides to take a bath!!!

## April 21

What we feed… grows!
So here are the rules ~
Feed the spirit positivity!
Feed the body healthy food!
Feed the heart unconditional love!
Feed the world kindness
and understanding!
…just a little 'food for thought!'

# April 22

I am remembering
and grateful today
for the sacrifice Jesus made to
save US from our sins!!
But somehow,
grateful doesn't seem enough!!
WHO will you SACRIFICE
something for today??
SPREAD THE LOVE!!

# April 23

I am thankful that
Jesus is the reason we can:
Rest in God's peace!!
Walk in God's grace!!
Live in God's righteousness!!
After all ~
ALL I have
is what God gives me!!
ALL I am
is what God made me!!
Faithfully forever, and
Thankful for each day
God gives me!!
Resting in the hands
that saved me!!
And now…
a day of REST and Gardening!!

# April 24

We would all be happier
if we GAVE more to others!
Learn to open your heart,
and give without expecting
anything in return.
Remember ~
there are two kinds of people in
the world: givers and takers.
The takers may eat better,
but the givers sleep better!!!
Your candle loses nothing
when it lights another...
Be generous today!

# April 25

Courage is letting go
of the familiar
to make a better future!!
At times, you must walk away
from the familiar
to fight for a brighter tomorrow!!
It helps to remember that
Hope gives you the strength,
Grace gives you the courage, and
Faith makes your day
worth living!!
Have a 'GO GET 'EM'
kind of day!

# April 26

When your back is against the
wall and when it seems
there is no way out.....
YOU have to face your
fears...Never give up!
Never back down!
Never lose Faith!
Be still and there will be
a gentle voice reminding you,
you are never alone!!
Give your struggles to God!

# April 27

You don't have to have certain
things happen in order to START
feeling better about your life ~
YOU just need to
FOCUS on the right things!!
You already have everything
YOU need to be, do and have
everything you want within you!!
Look inward today, see the good
and FOCUS on achieving
what YOU want!!!
It's an
'I CAN DO ANYTHING!!'
kind of day!!

# April 28

When you take the time to get to
know yourself, and
accept yourself
then you can learn to
LOVE yourself!!! After all, when
you know yourself,
you are empowered!!
When you accept yourself,
you are invincible!!
And when you LOVE yourself…
you are whole!!

# April 29

It's important to have someone
who listens to your worries,
thoughts and ideas… someone
who supports you in
ALL situations…
someone who is your strength
when yours is gone!
Now that's LOVE!
Look to the heavens and know
THIS is how God loves us!!

# April 30

Life is ALWAYS better when you have a sense of GRATITUDE, instead of entitlement!! Sometimes I just look up, smile and say, "I know that was you God! Thanks!" After all, everything happens because of Him!! Don't take the things in your life with attitude... Take them with Gratitude!

# May

## May 1

The world would be
a much better place if people
would pray as much as they talk...
prayer is so powerful, it's like
your own little bag of fairy dust...
so be a tinker bell and use it daily!
Let's try one together ~
"God, thank you for this
wonderful day you give us! Let us
use it for your will!! Amen!" ~
Now, don't you feel better?

## May 2

I want to say 'Thank You!'
and 'God Bless You!'
to all of those serving in the
military, past and present!!
Without you, we would not have
the freedoms we enjoy
every day of our lives!
We ALL need to remember ~
not every hero is a soldier, but
EVERY soldier is a hero!!
GOD BLESS AMERICA!!!

## May 3

Stop complaining that you don't
like how things are! Take control,
decide how YOU are going to
change it, think positively,
get rid of the drama, and
MOVE FORWARD!
Go have a great day!
Positive thoughts only!
I'm not going to sweat the
small stuff anymore...
I will not let anyone bring me
down today! Heck, with the right
amount of caffeine, even the Devil
runs for cover!

# May 4

Morning is God's way of saying:
"Live life one more time,
make a difference,
touch a heart, encourage a mind,
and inspire a soul."
Today is another wonderful day
full of positive energy and endless
possibilities!!
How will you LIVE it?

# May 5

Our words reveal our thoughts,
our manners mirror
our self-esteem,
our actions reflect our character,
and our habits predict the future!!
So take a close look at your
thoughts, manners, actions and
habits… because THEY reveal
who you are without words!
Hope everyone has a
THRILLING day!!

# May 6

In order to have VICTORY
in your future,
you must not become a VICTIM
of your past!!
Everything happens for a reason!!
Your past has made you who you
are today!!
Remember, a coincidence is just
God's way of performing a
miracle anonymously!!

## May 7

When your passion and purpose
are greater than
your fears and excuses,
you will find a way!!
Only two things motivate us…
fear of failure and
desire for success!!
Find your passion and you will
be successful!!

## May 8

I am reflecting on the story of
David and Goliath! Against what
seemed to be impossible odds,
with only a sling shot and
God on his side ~
David became a conqueror!!
Which reminds us ALL,
with God on our side,
who could stand against us?
Today be fearless, be faithful, and
become the CONQUERORS that
God intends us all to be!!

## May 9

In order to be
who you WANT to be,
it's best to concentrate on
who you are, instead of who
you're not!! Each of us was made
by God to be completely UNIQUE
and ONE OF A KIND!!
As Dr. Seuss said:
"Be who you are and
say what you feel, because
those who mind don't matter, and
those who matter, don't mind."

## May 10

I don't believe in that old cliché
that 'good things come to
those who wait!'
I think good things come
to those who want something
so bad they can't sit still!!
YOU are in control
of how you live each day and
what you accomplish!!
It's all about Focus and Faith!!!
Be the kind of person who makes
coffee nervous!!! LOL ~
Now pass the coffee and let's GO
MAKE IT a TERRIFIC DAY!!

## May 11

I love Matthew 7:7~
"Keep on asking, and you
will receive what you ask for.
Keep on seeking, and
you will find.
Keep on knocking, and the door
will be opened to you." ~
It's when we quit
that God can no longer help us!!
So Keep on trying and
Make it a WONDERFUL day!

## May 12

I wish a very Happy Mother's Day
to Margaret Gayle Locken-Petrilla
who has been my mother…
and my father.
I know that I was NOT an easy
child and so I thank you
for your sacrifices!!
All that I am and will be,
is because of you!!
I love you with all my heart!! ♥
HAPPY MOTHER'S DAY
EVERYONE!

## May 13

Isn't doing something
nice for others
so much more rewarding
than just thinking of ourselves?
I ask you ALL today,
reach out with a smile,
a handshake or a compliment!!
Make someone else
HAPPY today!!

## May 14

Don't regret ~
it holds a power over you
to cause fear of the unknown!
Things from the past
are what teach us about
having a better future!!
So learn and then live!!!
Besides, for every action
there is a consequence,
what goes around comes around!!
Karma will teach us all something,
whether we like it or not!!

# May 15

It takes a strong person
to know their faults,
a stronger one
to embrace their faults,
and a unbreakable person
to show their faults with pride!!
Be proud of who you are!!
YOU are a ONE OF KIND
creation by GOD!!
Have a blessed day, Y'all!!

## May 16

If you cannot keep your word,
then your integrity
as a person is worthless.
Realize that Integrity is
telling yourself the truth,
while Honesty is
telling the truth to other people.
I believe the best people have
BOTH Integrity AND Honesty for
others, as well as themselves!!
THAT is when you are a
GOOD person!!
Anything less is just a person!
Happy Glorious day, Y'all!!

## May 17

F.E.A.R. simply breaks down to:
Forget Everything And Run, or
Face Everything And Recover!!
The choice is ALL yours!!
Live by what you trust,
not by what you fear!!
Trust and Faith will always
lead you to where God wants you
to be!! Now, for a cup of coffee!
I wish EVERYONE a Happy
Terrific Day filled with LOVE!!

## May 18

I want to share Abe Lincoln's thoughts on happiness ~ "People are just as happy as they make up their minds to be!"
So, what will you make up YOUR mind to be or do today? Happiness is just a thought away!!

## May 19

I love Buddha's quote on sharing~
"Thousands of candles
can be lit from a single candle,
and the life of that candle
will not be shortened.
Happiness never decreases
by being shared!!!"
It costs you nothing
to share happiness
with another person!
Take today and
bring JOY to a stranger's life!
Now, for some COFFEE!! =))

## May 20

Until you realize
you are the creator
of your own misery
you will never be truly happy!!
For it is how you react
to any given situation
that brings you happiness!!
I have been reminded of that
this week and found
I am truly HAPPY!!
Happy Beautiful Day to
EVERYONE!!

## May 21

We are just like
flowers in a garden ~
we are all here to play our part
in making the world
a beautiful place!!
So bloom, spread your pedals and
touch someone's life today
in a Positive and Beautiful way!
And if it rains on your parade,
bring out the Slip 'n' Slide!

# May 22

I want you to
BELIEVE
you have wings!!
BELIEVE
that all things are possible!!
BELIEVE
in love!!
BELIEVE
that the climb is worth it!!
BELIEVE
in God and you will have it all!!

"Put on the full armor of God, so that you will be able to stand firm against the schemes of the devil."
~Ephesians 6:11

## May 23

The difference between
the impossible and the possible
lies in determination....
Determination and Discipline
are remembering what you want
and going for it!!
The only difference between
an opportunity and an obstacle
is your attitude!!
Go show the world
YOU CAN and YOU WILL!!

## May 24

I wish everyone a
Happy Memorial Day Weekend!
Please remember, it's not just
about BBQs and a day off work…
It's about our service men and
women who keep us safe and
make this a beautiful country!
God Bless America
and our military!!
Have a beautiful day, Y'all!! ♥

## May 25

Every situation has the
opportunity to
shake you or shape you!
It is up to you to decide which
way it will go. Take responsibility
for your part in it.
God puts people in your path
that need to be there.
Don't move out of the way
on your path… maybe you were
put there to help someone else!

## May 26

Gratefulness is the key
to a happy life
because if we are not grateful,
then no matter how much we have
we will not ever be happy!!
Here's your mantra today ~
A moment of gratitude makes a
difference in your attitude!! ~
Now go have a GORGEOUS,
GRATEFUL DAY!! ♥

## May 27

Most superheroes wear capes.
Well, my superhero wears combat
boots and camouflage uniforms.
For all the people who risk their
lives for our country…
THANK YOU!!
Freedom isn't free!
It's paid with the blood and sweat
of every SOLDIER
and the tears
of every person that loves them!
Thank them for their sacrifices!!
HAPPY MEMORIAL DAY
EVERYONE! ♥

## May 28

I believe we should remember
that what we feed grows!
Feed the mind positivity!
Feed the body healthy food!
Feed the heart unconditional love!
Feed the world
kindness and understanding!!
Have a beautiful Saturday, Y'all!!
♥

## May 29

Training yourself
to live in the present ~
without regretting the past
or fearing the future ~
is a recipe for a happy life!
Sometimes, in order to
open our eyes to the possibilities
of today and tomorrow, we have
to close our eyes on yesterday!!

# May 30

I am singing,
"Oh, what a beautiful morning...
oh, what a beautiful day,
it's the start of a
wonderful Morning, and a
cup of coffee is heading my way"
:)) LOLOL~
Hey… press 'Like' if you are
thinking 'She sounds Happy!'
Happiness is a CHOICE ~
Choose it with me!!

## May 31

We are all capable of
making a difference in others.
It may be in the words we speak
or a smile we give. ~
Giving in to the negativity within
you fuels the fire to destroy you…
instead, foster the strength and
support to which greater outcomes
can grow ~ Let your light shine. ♥

# June

# June 1

I know that the only one
who should judge us
has the amazing ability
to walk on water,
so why do those
who can't even swim
think they can judge others?
We should NEVER judge others
or look down at them!!
Embrace them,
and their differences!
You will be a much better person!!
Mathew 7:3~
"And why do you look at the
speck in your brother's eye, but
do not consider the plank in
your own eye?"
Agape, Y'all! ♥

## June 2

I believe that
Happiness keeps you Sweet,
Trials keep you Strong,
Sorrow keeps you Human,
Life keeps you Humble,
Success keeps you Growing,
But only FRIENDS
KEEP YOU GOING!!
I LOVE Y'ALL!! ♥

# June 3

I am still spinning with joy
from last night's party!!
THANK YOU so much
to ALL the beautiful women and
Dan who MADE last night...
AMAZING, WONDERFUL
and PERFECT!!!
My heart is bursting with love!!
And the Mavs WON!!!
Glorious Happy Monday,
Everyone!! ♥

# June 4

I believe that I can fly
because God made me to do so!!
Who will join me
in the beautiful skies
praising our maker?
"But those who trust in the Lord
will find new strength.
They will soar high
on wings like eagles."
~Isaiah 40:31
I wish EVERYONE a Beautifully
BLESSED day!! ♥

# June 5

I realize that I should have NO fears and NO worries, because ~ "The Lord is my light and my salvation, whom shall I fear. The lord is the strength of my life, of whom shall I be afraid."
~Psalms 27:1
F.E.A.R.=
False Evidence Appearing Real. Don't allow FEAR to keep you from what you are called to do!
Trust and Believe In
the One Who Called You!!
Have a Blessed day, Y'all!!

## June 6

I believe that if you limit
your choices only to what seems
possible or reasonable,
you disconnect yourself from what
you truly want, and all that is
left is a compromise.
It's only one little mark that
separates IMPOSSIBLE
from I'M POSSIBLE!!
Find your desire and ambition and
MAKE YOUR MARK!!
Happy Successful day to
EVERYONE ♥

## June 7

It's MY BIRTHDAY, so today take the time to CELEBRATE YOUR LIFE! SHINE for no reason! And LAUGH like no one is watching! Let's CELEBRATE!!

## June 8

If you spend ALL your time in
GRATITUDE, it's hard
to feel sad or depressed!
Sorrow and Joy
can't exist in the same space!
Try it!
BE GRATEFUL and LIVE!!

# June 9

I remember my grandmother
always being
the most peaceful person I knew!
When I would tell her I was
worried about something,
she would always tell me,
"worrying is simply NOT trusting
God!" TRUST, FAITH,
BELIEVE, ENCOURAGE and
LOVE ~
THAT is how she lived her life!
Her example BLESSES me
EVERYDAY!!
♥ Have a faithful day, Y'all!! ♥

## June 10

I know that complaining
does not change anything!
The negativity only
brings YOU down and
makes people not
want to be around you!
Count your blessings instead!!
And don't forget to ~
Carry a heart that never hates.
Carry a smile that never fades.
Carry a touch that never hurts, and
life will be GREAT! ♥

## June 11

Life is NOT a competition!
If that is how you are living,
you will never be happy!
Choose instead to enjoy life and
all it has to offer YOU!
When you spend your time
focused on what others have,
you are not appreciating or being
grateful for what you DO have!
God will only give you more
when you are GRATEFUL!!
Have an AWESOME day, Y'all!!
♥

# June 12

"Love bears all things,
believes all things,
hopes all things,
endures all things.
Love never fails."
~1 Corinthians 13:7-8
Today, I wish for everyone to find
THIS kind of LOVE!
Unconditional, Never-ending, and
Always present!
God's love is always the answer!!
Happy Loving day!! ♥

## June 13

If you are waiting
for someone else to 'rescue' you
or 'take care' of you,
then you will never be happy!!
Until you stand
on your own two feet and
take responsibly for your own life,
you will NEVER truly know how
strong you really are!!
BELIEVE IN YOURSELF~
it shows others they should, too!!
Happy Glorious
'Go conquer the WORLD!'
Day…
But first, COFFEE!! ♥

**June 14**

Problems are just opportunities
that you haven't found
the answer to!
Change your perspective
and life gets a lot easier!!
It takes little thought or effort
to be negative and complain.
Praise, happiness, and joy
comes from within,
as we dwell on God's grace,
goodness, and blessings!!
Make it a Joyful day, Y'all!! ♥

## June 15

I wonder if anyone
has ever realized
there is only one letter difference
between the words
TRUTH and TRUST?
Maybe it's because,
one leads to the other!!
Remember ~ beautiful words
aren't always truthful and truthful
words aren't always beautiful…
and trust is like a mirror..
once it's broken, we can never
look at it the same again!
Today, be truthful and
trustworthy!!
Have a Wonderful day, Y'all!!

# June 16

Any man can father a child…
but it takes a REAL man
to be a Father!!
HAPPY FATHER'S DAY
to all of those men out there
that are man enough
to step up to the plate!
A daughter's connection
with her dad sets the rules for how
she will allow men to treat her!
Today ~ I say "Thank YOU,
Grandpa, for making me believe I
deserve happiness!!" ♥

## June 17

I believe that singing
a happy song lightens your heart
and your mind,
so sing it with me…
"oh what a beautiful morning...
oh what a beautiful day,
it's the start of a wonderful
Monday, and a cup of coffee is
heading my way!!"

## June 18

The happiest people
don't have it all, they just make
the best of what they've got!!
When you spend your time
being grateful,
it's hard to be unhappy!!
Have a SUPER day, Y'all!! ♥

## June 19

We are all capable
of making a difference in others!!
It may be in the words we speak
or a smile we give.
So today, give care and thought
of how YOU can make
someone else HAPPY
today and feel the joy
in yourself rise as well!!
Go make someone SMILE!! ♥

## June 20

It's a new start
to a new week
full of fresh opportunities and
another chance to dig in and
go for your dreams!
Simply adjust your attitude to
POSITIVE
and don't forget to
laugh along the way!!
Never stop striving to be better
than who you were yesterday!

# June 21

We should not dwell on the past,
it will only get you behind.
The future has not yet come,
so in this present,
strive for that future and
learn from your past!
Too many people hold on to the
bad and let it weigh them down!
DON'T!!
If you spend your time looking at
what you left behind,
you WILL miss what is
waiting for you ahead!!
Go find your HAPPINESS today
by making someone else
HAPPY!!! ♥

**June 22**

When we look at others, we
should not envy
or be jealous
because that is the
wrong direction to focus!
Look in the mirror and
REALIZE…
God created you,
a true ONE OF A KIND!!
There is no one else
EXACTLY like you!
Now focus on your uniqueness
and your positive qualities and
go out and SHINE today!!
Make God proud!! ♥

# June 23

If everything in life
was easy, there would be
no need for dedication,
perseverance or commitment.
So don't be so quick to
throw in the towel,
but rather use it to wipe the sweat
from your brow as you try harder
to conquer the situation!!
Remember:
To win the race, don't look back!
Don't let your trials and failures
hold you back from finishing the
greatest race EVER!

## June 24

Too many people
USE their past and what has
happened to them as crutches!
Well that's poop!
Learn from it!
Discover your strength from it!
There are people who have RISEN
from serious tragedy and made
something GREAT of themselves!
It's your choice ~ sit and blame
your past for who you aren't, or
take responsibility and become
who you want to be TODAY!!
Be who GOD wants you to be!!
Be UNIQUE!! ♥

# June 25

Three thoughts for the day…
~Wisdom is not about having all
of the answers,
it's knowing that you never will!!
~A beautiful appearance will last a
few decades, but a beautiful
personality will last a lifetime!!
AND THE BIGGEST ONE…
~Kindness costs nothing...
BUT can reward you so MUCH!

# June 26

"Do your best
to live with everyone
in peace!!"
~Romans 12:18
Have a Super Blessed Day,
EVERYONE!! ♥

## June 27

I wonder if you know
what it is that you want out of life?
Have you asked yourself
that question?
Did you find your answer? Then
WHAT are you waiting for? It's a
new week, new chances,
new choices and
new opportunities!!
Now GO MAKE IT HAPPEN!!!
Happy Magical day, Y'all!! ♥

## June 28

With COURAGE,
you will dare to take risks, have
the strength to be compassionate,
and the wisdom to be humble!
Courage is the foundation
of integrity!!
Remember ~ Challenges aren't
there to stop you… they're there
to help you grow!!
So for today, be courageous and
accept a new challenge,
or answer an old one!!

## June 29

Inner peace begins
the minute you choose
not to allow another person,
place or thing control your
emotions in negative ways!
Stay in control
of your reactions and responses!
LOVE, FAITH and HOPE are the
strongest and most powerful
emotions ~ God has love for you,
faith in you and hope for you…
ALWAYS!!

# June 30

We should NEVER allow others
to make our path for us!!
It is YOUR road and yours alone!
Others may walk it with you,
but no one can walk it for you!
And with every step
you take forward, you gain
strength to take another!!
Just repeat ~ "I choose to be the
best that I can be! I choose to be
courageous in everything I do! My
past doesn't dictate who I am! The
choice is MINE!!" Now go
"choose" to be GREAT!! ♥

# July

# July 1

Giving in to the
negativity within you
fuels the fire that will destroy you!
Instead, foster the
strength and support to which
greater outcomes can grow!!
There is something positive in you
and in your life!
FIND IT!
FOCUS ON IT!
And MAKE IT GROW!!!

## July 2

We should all learn
to appreciate
those we have in our lives
on a DAILY basis!
Appreciation is just
another form of love!
Learn to realize the value
of those in your life because
once they are gone… it's too late!
Tell someone in your life today
how much they mean to you!!
Happy day, Y'all!! ♥
Now, where's the coffee?
LOL

# July 3

If you are making plans
for your life, make sure to
include God's plans for you!
No one wants you to succeed
MORE than he does!!
"For I know what I have planned
for you says the Lord. I have plans
to prosper you not to harm you.
I have plans to give you
a future filled with hope."
~Jeremiah 29:11
Have a BLESSED day, Y'all!!
♥

# July 4

On our Independence Day,
contemplate this ~
you'll never realize how strong
you are until you have no other
choice but to be strong!!
"America, God shed his grace on
thee, and crown thy good
with brotherhood
...from sea to shining sea!"
God Bless those who
keep us FREE!
Happy Birthday, America!

## July 5

I know it's a short week
so there's no time to waste!!
Remember ~ every success starts
with a plan of action to get there ~
small steps emanate
strong results!!
So grab some coffee and
Let's get to planning!!!
Happy day, Y'all!! ♥

## July 6

GOD made each of us an
ORIGINAL MASTERPIECE!!
Don't let anyone
turn you into a copy!!
Now go show the world
your amazing colors and
let your unique beauty SHINE!!
Happy Day, Y'all!!
Don't forget, to have faith in
others, you MUST have faith in
yourself first and you can find that
by having faith in GOD!!

## July 7

No one can go back and
create a new beginning.
But EVERYONE can start now
and create a new ending!!
Your destiny lies in your choices!!
We often meet our fate
on the road we took to avoid it!!
So start committing to
YOURSELF!!
Today is a new day
to make new choices and
take new chances!!
Happy day, Y'all!! ♥

## July 8

Although you may not be able
to control certain situations in
your life, you can control how you
CHOOSE to deal with them!
Changing one thing for the better
is worth MORE than proving a
thousand things that are wrong!!
Just remember ~
some people want it to happen,
some wish it would happen,
others MAKE IT happen!
Which one are you?
Go MAKE it a FABULOUS
DAY!!! ♥

## July 9

"And when you pray,
do not be like the hypocrites,
for they love to pray standing in
the synagogues and on the street
corners to be seen by others."
~Matthew 6:5
Instead, have a
personal relationship with God!!
Let him in your heart and
your heart will never need
for anything!!
Have a blessed day, Y'all!!
♥

**July 10**

You begin the journey
toward success
by following
two simple rules~
1. Get started, and
2. Don't quit!!!
Have a SUPER DAY,
Y'ALL!!
♥

## July 11

Remember ~ "I am"
two of the most powerful words
in the world,
for whatever we put after them
becomes our reality!!!
It's never too late
to be who you thought you'd be!!
Today start with ~ I am… and
then add YOUR positive ending!!
I AM READY
TO ROCK THIS DAY!! ♥

# July 12

In LIFE, you get
what you give!
If you don't like
what you're getting,
then look at what you are giving.
Don't just sit and complain
about what you are NOT getting!
It is often those who give little
that want the most! Remember…
"Do unto others as you would
have them do unto you."
~Luke 6:31
Now GO MAKE IT a TERRIFIC
GIVING DAY!!
♥

## July 13

When you allow things
to bother you,
you are giving them
power over you!
Try to remove the emotions
and march forward and do what
you must to stay in control!
Many people consider IQ the only
form of intelligence, but EQ is
almost as important!!
When you can maintain
Emotional Intelligence
in the middle of a storm ~
YOU ARE WINNING!!!

## July 14

I pray that you never
underestimate
the power of words,
for they can be more lethal
than a shot gun
or more healing
than a mother's kiss!!
Please watch the video
"The Power of Words"
on my page!
And please use your words today
to make a
POSITIVE DIFFERENCE in
someone's life!!

## July 15

It doesn't matter where
LIFE takes YOU-
It matters were YOU take LIFE!!
Make the best of everyday
and remember ~
Respect is earned.
Honesty is appreciated.
Trust is gained.
Loyalty is returned.
Have a FABULOUS DAY,
Y'ALL!!! ♥

# July 16

We should ALL try to
be givers, not takers!!
It's really simple…
Listen more,
Talk less,
Compliment more,
Criticize less,
Forgive more,
Judge less!!
I promise that, in the end, you will
be happy more
and not friend-less!!!
Today give a hand UP to a
stranger and not down!!
Make it a GIVING day, Y'all!! ♥

## July 17

If you feel uncomfortable with
where life has taken you,
remember the hand of GOD will
not lead you where the hand of
GOD will not protect you!
Accept the new experience and
rise to the challenge of growing
in the direction that
God wants you to go!
"For he will command his
angels concerning you
to guard you in all your ways."
~Psalm 91:11
Have a BLESSED DAY, Y'all!!

## July 18

True happiness
is the spiritual experience
of living every minute
with love, grace and gratitude!!
Love yourself, your life,
and those around you!
Be graceful in your approach
and response to every
experience in your life!
And ALWAYS be grateful for
EVERYTHING in your life.
It could ALL be gone in a flash!!

## July 19

The difference between
school and life is that
in school, you're taught a lesson
and then given a test.
In life, you're given a test
that teaches you a lesson!
Remember ~ Life isn't about
what happens to you,
it's about
how you handle what happens!!

## July 20

I am remembering
when I would bring my worries
to my grandma, she would always
say, "Worrying is just a lack of
FAITH! Go talk to God!"
Then she would give me one of
her grandma hugs that
made everything ok!
Today, Choose to have FAITH!
Choose to be strong!!
Choose to be a winner!!
I'll see you on
the mountain of FAITH!!

## July 21

Neither genius, fame, nor love
can show the greatness of the soul!
Only kindness can do that!!
Kindness is not meant
to be paid back,
it is meant to be passed on!!
Take a moment today to
be KIND to a stranger!
You might just change their day
or even their life!!
KINDNESS ~ PASS IT ON!!

## July 22

Too many people
make excuses as to why
their lives aren't happy!
Well, I believe that when your
passion and purpose
are greater than
your fears and excuses,
you will find happiness!!
Let go of the excuses and jump
into life with PASSION!!

## July 23

TREAT people
the way you want to be treated ~
TALK to people
the way you want to be talked to!
If you find someone isn't giving
you what you need,
maybe you should fine tune
what you are giving them!
Respect will get you RESPECT!

# July 24

I want share a bible quote ~
"Be joyful always, pray continually, and give thanks in all circumstances, for this is God's will for you in Christ Jesus"
~1 Thessalonians 5:16-18
Sounds like easy instructions!
Today I give thanks to the Lord for my Joyous life... Amen!
Have a BLESSED & JOYOUS DAY, Y'all!!

## July 25

I love that each new day
brings the excitement of
what's to come,
the possibilities are endless!!
My eyes are wide open
and accepting of the future
and all that it holds!
Remember, if you can imagine it,
then there's always a possibility to
make it happen!!

## July 26

It's time to get your heads
on straight, your hearts in the
right place, and your smiles on
your sweet faces!!
Remember, a positive attitude
causes a chain reaction of positive
thoughts, events and outcomes!
It is a catalyst, a spark that creates
extraordinary results!
Now let's get out there and
change the world!! ♥

## July 27

It's not about
where you've been
or who you are.
It's about where you're going
and who you will be!!
The future is full of hope and
promise if you want it to be!!
Today could be the first day of
change ~ It's ALL up to YOU!!
Have a WONDERFUL DAY and
I'll see you at the top of the
mountain!! ♥

# July 28

Everyone goes through life
with their hand out.
The choice is,
is your hand out
to TAKE - or to GIVE?
You decide!
The difference creates
joy or misery
not only in your life
but in those around you as well!
Today choose to GIVE HELP
to a stranger!
I promise it will make YOU
feel even better
than the ones you help!

## July 29

Success is having
the courage,
determination, and the will
to DO IT!!
Failure is making excuses
why you didn't succeed
and blaming others around you
for your failure!
I will promise you this ~
One risk
is worth a thousand dreams!!

# July 30

Attention!
Happiness has arrived
in full force!
Please be advised
that there is a slight chance
of sleeping in,
and the possibility of enjoying it!
…followed by delicious coffee
and the best part... A DAY OFF!!
Remember it's ok to celebrate the
goodness of God!!
Just don't forget to say
"Thank You!"
Happy day, Y'all!!
Enjoy!! ♥

## July 31

Every action you take
is a seed you sow,
and every seed you sow
is a harvest you'll reap!
You'll never change your life
until you change your choices!
So today, keep your heart
and mind open
because God wants to do
something
in and through you!

# August

# August 1

The moment you settle for less,
is the moment you get less
than you settled for!!
Look at yourself
in the mirror and say ~
"I deserve GREAT things!"
Then go out and
MAKE THEM HAPPEN!!
The opportunities are there,
but we must make room
for them in our lives!!
Believe in YOU
and others will follow!!

## August 2

How can you go forward
in your life if you are always
looking in the past?
You Can't!!
Today… MOVE forward!!
No more looking back!!
Those who are gone
from our lives,
we can wish many blessings for!!
And those who are in our future,
we should be excited to meet!!!
FOCUS
on where you want to be…
not where you have been!

## August 3

It takes more energy
to be negative
than to be positive.
I'd rather waste my energy
on something…
or someone wonderful!!
And if you need a little help
today getting in a GREAT mood,
try music!!
Today's theme song is posted and
I highly encourage
YOU to SING ALONG!!
Go MAKE IT a WOW
Wednesday!! ♥

## August 4

The worth of a person
is not in what they own
or how much they make,
yet in how much they give,
without need for a thing in return!
After all, our significance
will not be found in the
advancement of self, but in
our impact on others!
Today, try and be the positive
difference in someone's life!!
Give Freely and the rewards
fill your soul!!

## August 5

I believe…
we do not become HAPPY
because we are successful;
we become successful
because we are HAPPY!!
When you are a happy,
positive person,
you see life
in a different way!
No valley too big!
No mountain too high!!
Let go of the negative and
REACH FOR THE STARS!!!

## August 6

It doesn't quite matter
who you were a decade ago,
a year ago, or even yesterday...
what matters is who you are today,
and will be tomorrow!!
So for today, without reservation,
LET GO of the past!!
And START being the person
YOU want to be TODAY!!

# August 7

Remember…
"Only what comes from you
can come back to you."
~Proverbs 11:24
So think about what you
PUT into the world…
what you give and
how you treat others!
For in life, IT ALL
COMES BACK TO YOU!!
Give to others with gentle hands!
Live with a grateful attitude!
Love with a kind heart!

## August 8

Today is a new, clean slate
to set your dreams upon
and create a new path on
how to make them happen!!
Don't let anyone
stand in your way
and don't let the doubters
convince you to quit!
BELIEVE IN YOURSELF, and
GO MAKE IT HAPPEN!!
Remember to be the
Author of your Destiny, not the
Victim of your Circumstance!!!

## August 9

I believe… that you are
what you think!
Be careful where
you let your mind dwell,
for it will either bring success
or failure!!
Think it today!
Become it tomorrow!!
Nothing can help you
or hurt you
as much as the thoughts
you carry in your head!
Now say it OUT LOUD!!
"I will be..."

# August 10

We need to be careful of how
our FOCUS
AFFECTS US!!
Good or bad,
what you focus on
affects your thoughts!
What you think about
affects your feelings!!
How you feel
will affect you, and
everyone around you!!!
So today, focus on
POSITIVE possibilities
AND you will have
more AMAZING opportunities!!!
Now grab your coffee and let's
MAKE this day WONDERFUL!!!
♥

## August 11

Things happen in life,
whether you're ready or not!
Seize the moment
and take a chance...
or spend the rest of your life
not ever knowing!
After all, the measure of a person
is not on how well they
prepare for everything to go right,
but how gracefully they stand up
and move on
when everything goes wrong!!
Today~ TAKE THE CHANCE!!
♥

# August 12

Knowledge…
is knowing when you can't.
Faith…
is knowing that God can!!
Wisdom…
is finding a solution in chaos!
Courage…
is making a change
even through the fear!!
Have a COURAGEOUS and
FAITHFUL Day!!!
Now, let's grab some coffee and
get ready for the day!! =))

# August 13

If you never chase what you want,
you'll never get it!!
If you never ask,
then the answer is always no!!
If you never step forward,
you'll always be
in the same place!!
So let the CHASE begin!!
Find the ANSWERS
to your questions, and
TAKE THE FIRST STEP
towards what you want from life!!
Have a SUPER
SUCCESSFUL DAY!! ♥

## August 14

Sometimes, what we don't do
is every bit as powerful
as what we do!!
And what we don't say
speaks louder than any words!!
Not only does this keep you
at a higher level of grace,
but both actions
provoke thoughts in others!!
It's the simple rule ~
Treat others as you would have
them treat you!!

## August 15

Today's simple thought
is to remind everyone ~
Be yourself… not
what everyone wants you to be!!
When you attempt to be
something you are not
or think you are better
than anyone else ~
YOU LOOSE!!!
God created us ALL to be
ONE OF A KIND works of ART!!
We each SHINE and SPARKLE
in our own SPECIAL way!!
And when we work together ~
WE SHINE BRIGHTER!!

# August 16

You should be kind
to people on your way up…
you never know when you might
need them on your way down!!
Love, Kindness, Compassion,
Forgiveness, and Understanding
are the most precious of gifts that
God gives us
to share with others...
it's up to us to share them!

# August 17

I believe that…
every choice you make
has an end result.
Every beginning has an end.
Every action has a reaction.
Life comes with consequences!
So remember to be happy
with what you have,
grateful for what you are given,
and never want
more than you need!!
Now go have a WILD DAY
and try to help someone else
along the way!! ♥

# August 18

Only by facing the Darkness
with an OPEN heart,
will you truly be able to
see the Light...
for it is only through Faith
that we can truly be at peace!!
Instead of
judging and condemning,
try helping and healing!
When you do... you will find
AMAZING ABUNDANT
LOVE!!
Have a Compassionate day,
Y'all!! ♥

# August 19

I'm starting today with a prayer ~
"May the words from my mouth,
and the thoughts from my mind
be acceptable to you, O Lord,
My Rock, My Defender!!"
Remember that a simple
compliment or smile can
REALLY change someone's day!!
Wouldn't it feel GREAT to know
YOU CREATED HAPPINESS
in someone else?
Now let's start this day
by complimenting people
and smiling!!

# August 20

I love that today
is another wonderful day
full of positive energy and
endless possibilities!
Remember,
"Only what comes from you
can come back to you!"
~Proverbs 11:24
So go spread love, joy and
kindness today!!
Hope EVERYONE has a
SUPER DAY!! ♥

**August 21**

I am so happy today
for two reasons~
1st: It's Tiffany Hendra's
BIRTHDAY (I love her!!) and
2nd: it's Bible Verse Day! ~
"Have I not commanded thee? Be
strong and of a good courage,
be not afraid nor dismayed,
for the Lord thy God is with thee
whithersoever thou goest"
~Joshua 1:9
Have a BLESSED and
HAPPY Day, EVERYONE!! ♥

## August 22

Woke up today and realized...
it's time to ROCK!!
A new week,
full of new opportunities and
new possibilities!!
Look back ONLY to learn...
then find a new way to get
what you want and GO FOR IT!!
Get motivated by your passion and
take the steps that will take you
towards success!!

## August 23

What we don't do
is every bit as powerful
as what we do!!
And what we don't say
speaks louder than any words!!
Both actions provoke
thoughts in others!
Communication is the key to a
happy and healthy relationship
with those you value!!
For the devil lies in the confusion
waiting for a chance!!
It's ok to SPEAK your mind…
just be gentle with your words!

## August 24

I know how powerful
our words can be!!
Every time words are spoken,
SOMETHING is created ~
Be conscious of what you say
and how you say it ~
Use words that build up,
appreciate, encourage and inspire!
Not just to others,
but to YOURSELF as well!!
Let's start with "Today, I am...."
and you fill in the rest
POSITIVELY!!

# August 25

Life may not always
send you easy choices,
but it's the way you handle them
that really counts!!
After all, STRENGTH is obtained
by overcoming obstacles.
Life is going to knock you down
and try to keep you down!
It's up to YOU to find strength,
GET UP and KEEP LIVING!!
So grab your coffee and
LET'S MAKE THIS DAY
SHINE!!! ♥

# August 26

Three simple words…
FAITH, HOPE, and LOVE!
Every day is a great day to
HAVE FAITH,
GIVE HOPE,
and SHOW your LOVE
to the people around you!!
You never know ~
Today might be your last chance
to do it OR it might
change someone's life
for the better!!
Be THAT person today!!
Wishing EVERYONE a
FABULOUS DAY!! ♥

## August 27

Today's thought is simple,
but I REALLY
want you to HEAR IT!!
Just in case no one
has told you today...
YOU MATTER!!!
Wishing EVERYONE an
AMAZINGLY HAPPY Day!! :~))

## August 28

If God brings you to it,
then he will see you through it!
Some situations are not meant
for you to change.
Some situations are meant
to change you!
We must try to figure out
the difference!!
After all, God will become
more in us
when we become
less in ourselves!!
Hope EVERYONE has a
BLESSED day!! ♥

## August 29

Here's a little quote
to get you going today ~
"Patience and perseverance
have a magical effect
before which difficulties disappear
and obstacles vanish."
So today I am wishing everyone
a healthy dose of
PATIENCE and
PERSEVERANCE!!
Go show the WORLD
how it's done!!

## August 30

On my trip to Washington,
I saw the most amazing
sign of PERSISTENCE!
There, a little pine tree
grew from a solid mass of rock.
No one told the tree he couldn't,
SO HE DID!!!
Courage isn't always a ROAR!
Sometimes… it's the quiet
whisper saying,
"YOU CAN DO IT!!"
So today, go out and
show the world....
YOU CAN DO ANYTHING!!
Make it a PERSISTENT DAY!!!
♥

# August 31

Reminding everyone…
Don't miss your opportunity to
make a difference EVERY day!!
Touch someone's heart!!
Encourage a mind!!
And lead someone to become
what they aspire to be!!
Creating GOOD in the world
brings GOOD to YOU!!
Be the POSITIVE
you want to see!!
Happy Day, Y'all!
I'm off to work early
and I will miss chatting
with Y'all today!
I'll answer on my first break!!
SHINE ON!!

# September

## September 1

Want to remind everyone…
that you must know weakness,
so you can know strength…
know sadness,
so you can know happiness…
know heartbreak,
so you can know love…
and know yourself,
so you can feel pride!
Tough times never last,
but tough people DO!!
Keep your eyes up to the heavens
and KNOW~
YOU ARE LOVED!!
Hope Y'all have
a KNOWING day!! ♥

## September 2

Happiness is not defined
by your profession
or economic status. . .
happiness is defined
by how much YOU love others
and are loved
by your family and friends!!
Have a LOVING DAY Y'ALL!!

**HAPPY LABOR DAY!!**

## September 3

Any fool can criticize,
condemn, and complain…
and most fools do!!
But it takes CHARACTER
and SELF-CONTROL
to be understanding
and forgiving!!
Be THAT person today!!
Be the one who walks
in the other person's shoes
and forgives their weaknesses!!
Have a SENSATIONAL DAY!! ♥

## September 4

Today, here is a
simple but honest quote
from C.S. Lewis~
"I BELIEVE IN GOD like
I believe in the sunrise…
not because I can see it,
but because I can see
all that it touches."
We don't have to see things
to believe in them,
it's OUR CHOICE!!
But I will say,
BELIEVING and FAITH
gets me through
ALL of my tough times!!

## September 5

I want to remind you today to
clear out the clutter in your heart,
your mind and your home...
Make room for the good things,
the things WORTHY
of being in your life!
If your life is
too stuffed
with unimportant things
there is no room to grow!!
Let go of the negative clutter and
see what wonderful things
it opens up your life to!!

## September 6

Your day will be even better
if you start with positivity!!
So smile, be happy,
be optimistic and be positive!
And remember that
every time words are spoken,
something is created.
Be conscious of what you say
and how you say it.
Use words that build up,
appreciate, encourage and inspire
EVERYONE…
including YOU!!

## September 7

Life isn't complicated,
WE make it complicated
by the choices WE make!!
The choice to DO GOOD
will CREATE GOOD!
The choice to offer KINDNESS
will bring KINDNESS!!
For today, use your smile
to change the world,
DON'T let the world
change your smile!!!
Be the light and shine a path!!

## September 8

It takes courage
to stand out
but nothing to fit in!
Be who you are!!
Your life is yours
and determined by the Lord,
NOT anyone else!!
Focus on doing GOOD
and GOOD will happen!!
Let go of sorrow and hurt
and SHOW KINDNESS
everywhere you go!!
SHINE like the STAR
God created you to be!!
(and crank up the wattage!!!)

## September 9

We should ALL
begin each new day
as if it is
the beginning of our life,
for it truly is the beginning
of what is left of our lives!!
Be positive, stay happy,
don't let the negativity or
drama of the world get you down!!
SMILE!
Today is your gift from God!
What you do with today
is your gift to God!!

**September 10**

You can never become
the person you want to be
if you don't start acting
like the person
you want to become!!
Those who wait for
the 'perfect' opportunity
will soon see the future
become their past!
DON'T WAIT!!
Make the choice TODAY and
BELIEVE that
all things are possible!!
The reality is~
when you know yourself,
you are empowered,
but when you accept yourself…
you are invincible!!!

## September 11

Today, I am asking
that as we all remember
the heartbreaking, vicious attack
that took 2974 human lives…
know that,
within our sorrow and tears,
we are a STRONGER NATION
and PEOPLE for surviving!
Notice how we ALL
pulled together…
ignoring race, religion, status
and age to
HELP ONE ANOTHER
when we needed it the most!
NO hatred or evil can stop us
when have such strong
LOVE in our hearts!!
STAY STRONG!!
God Bless us ALL!! ♥

# September 12

Today…
watch what you meditate on
or think about!
If you focus on problems,
they WILL get bigger…
but if you
FOCUS ON POSSIBILITIES,
then you will find your answers!
"I will think myself HAPPY"
~the Apostle Paul
How will YOU
'think' yourself today?
Don't wait to see
what kind of day it's going to be~
DECIDE NOW
what kind of day it WILL BE!
Happy MIRACLE DAY!! ♥

# September 13

Life should NOT be a
competition with others,
but with yourself!
Challenge yourself to
BE BETTER and DO BETTER
every day!
We are each UNIQUE works
that should NEVER be compared!
We can EACH be
an AMAZING BLESSING,
if we CHOOSE to!!
After all,
compromise and compassion
are better than
competition and conflict!!
Now let's grab some
STRONG COFFEE and have a
TERRIFIC DAY!!! ♥

# September 14

In order to move forward,
we must be willing
to let go of the past
to make a better future!
The PAST will hold you back
from good things
standing in your face!
Remember…
to search for new oceans,
you have to be willing
to lose sight of the shoreline!
Have FAITH that what lies ahead
is meant for your HAPPINESS!!
Now sing it with me,
"I got to keep on Movin'!!!"

## September 15

One of the best things in life
is to be is REAL!
Be who and what
God created you to be
not what others want you to be!!
Real people aren't perfect!
Perfect people aren't real!!
Learn to look for the good things,
without expecting perfection!
Learn to accept people
for who they are!!
REAL happiness only comes to
REAL people!!
Make today shine!!

## September 16

Don't listen to people
who say "You can't!"
They have given up and
have forgotten that it's just a little
mark that separates
Impossible from I'm Possible!!
Stand your ground and
KEEP SHINING!!

## September 17

If you are not completely open,
honest and truthful with yourself,
you never can be with others.
I have always been a
STRONG believer in
'THE TRUTH
SHALL SET YOU FREE!'
Lies are like chains
that hold you down ~ break free!!
Remember…
you don't have to be PERFECT,
YOU just have to be YOU!!
Each of us are
AMAZINGLY UNIQUE
and are worthy of LOVE,
COMPASSION and HONESTY!!

# September 18

Your biggest trials
sometimes come right before
your biggest breakthroughs.
Stay ENCOURAGED
and FAITHFUL
and know that your 'test' will
indeed be a powerful 'testimony!'
At the end of the day,
it's up to us to choose
to focus on what tears us apart
or what holds us together!
FOCUS on the POSITIVE and
put only GOOD into the world!!
After all, A little rain can
straighten a flower stem and
a little love can change a life…
CHANGE A LIFE!

## September 19

You should not allow the
road blocks that enter your path
to become your dead end in life.
If you find yourself in a situation
you can't change,
then change your reaction
to that situation.
Then the solution
will become clear!
Above ALL, remember ~
You can't go wrong
doing the right thing!!
GO GET YOUR MIRACLE!! ♥

## September 20

I want everyone to try this today...
EXPECT - nothing of anyone!
ACCEPT - others as they are!
RESPECT - everyone regardless!
CONTROL - yourself because it's
all in your control!
Now let's get to making
THIS DAY Sparkle and SHINE
like only WE CAN!!!
Happy TERRIFIC DAY!!!
WHERE'S THE COFFEE??
LOL ♥

# September 21

Today I wanted to be reminded of
what LOVE is
and how it behaves!
I went to the 'Good Book' and
read the following ~
"Love is patient, love is kind.
It does not envy, it does not boast,
it is not proud.
It does not dishonor others,
it is not self-seeking,
it is not easily angered,
it keeps no record of wrongs."
~1 Corinthians 13:4-5
THIS is how LOVE should be,
whether it is with
a STRANGER or a FRIEND!!
Today, let's ALL
practice REAL LOVE!! ♥
Have a WONDERFUL LOVING
DAY, EVERYONE!!

## September 22

We shouldn't judge a good day
by the happiness we take from it!!
We should judge it
by the happiness we bring into it!!
It's OUR CHOICE
to MAKE this a
HAPPY, WONDERFUL DAY!!
So who's with me?
Make a stranger smile or laugh
and LEAVE HAPPINESS
everywhere you go today!!

## September 23

I believe that YOU
are where you are
because of who you were
but where you go
depends entirely
on who you choose to be!!!
Now, SING it with me~
'Oh What a beautiful morning...
oh what a beautiful day,
it's the start of a wonderful
morning, and a cup of coffee is
heading my way!!'

## September 24

Everyday, I learn something new
about the world,
but more so about me...
and sometimes, in order to find
real peace and happiness,
I just have to simply let go!!
Let go of EVERYTHING
holding you back or down!
Reach for HAPPINESS and
be sure to ONLY ADD GOOD
to the world!!
The choice is yours!
Today… Be the DIFFERENCE
you want to see!! ♥

## September 25

In the midst of any turmoil
in my life, when I experience
a peace that can't be explained,
it's at that moment I realize that
someone is praying for me!!
Because it's not about
what religion you are!
It's not a religion,
It's a RELATIONSHIP!!
If we have that relationship, then
WE ARE ALL
ON THE SAME TEAM!!
Today pray for a stranger and
experience PEACE!! ♥

## September 26

When you surround yourself
with good people
there can only be good outcomes!
Today's goal is to
'THINK POSITIVELY!'
Now let's all say it together,
'Nothing is going to
get me down today and
I WILL think positively.'
Because the TRUTH is
that the only difference
between an
opportunity and an obstacle
is your ATTITUDE!!!

## September 27

We should welcome
every morning with a smile!
Look on the new day
as a special gift,
a golden opportunity
to complete what you were unable
to finish yesterday!
We should challenge
the impossible,
explore beyond our comfort zone,
refuse to be limited by boundaries
and never settle for less
than we deserve!!
Now let's go MAKE IT a
TERRIFIC DAY!! ♥

## September 28

If we set our mind
in the right direction,
our bodies will follow!
Watch what you FOCUS on!!
Don't allow the negative
to creep in!
STAY POSITIVE and
your results will be POSITIVE!!
Today… FOCUS ON
THE GOOD YOU CAN GIVE
to the world!!

## September 29

I believe… you should turn
your dreams into goals!
Turn your goals into projects!
Turn your projects into plans!
Turn your plans into actions...
Only then, will your actions lead
you to your dreams!!
So what are
YOUR GOALS today?
I'm starting with COFFEE!!

**September 30**

I'm thanking God
not only for today
but
every day
that I can continue to live!
One thing I know FOR SURE~
when we're grateful,
there is no time to be hateful...
gratitude is the attitude
of the blessed!
So remember to
focus on the GOOD
and have a very blessed and
FABULOUS DAY!!! ♥

# October

## October 1

Challenges aren't there
to stop you...
They are there to see if you
have the courage to defeat them!
Success is waiting
for those who are ready to persist
and face the obstacles in their path
with a positive attitude!
So what will you do
in the face of a challenge today?
Let nothing stop you
until your dreams come true!!

## October 2

The Light of God surrounds You!
The Love of God enfolds You!
The Power of God protects You!
And the Presence of God
watches over You!!
Wherever You are, God Is!!!
Today I give a
HEARTFELT 'THANK YOU'
to God for ALL that is my life!!
What are you
GRATEFUL for today?
Focus on gratitude and it will
change your attitude!!

## October 3

Mistakes make us human!
Failures make us stronger!
Love keeps us alive!
And gratitude keeps us humble!
For in the end, we must realize
that life was a gift and
how we chose to live
was our gift back!
Choose today
to make your gift one of
FAITH, HOPE and LOVE!!
And don't forget to sprinkle it
with KINDNESS!! ♥

## October 4

Rise n' Shine!
It's a new day!
Take the time to appreciate and be
thankful for what you have today!!
It's not where you've been
or who you are.
It's about where you're going
and who you will be.
The future is full of hope
and promise if you want it to be!!
So set your goals and
let's go MAKE IT HAPPEN!!
Have a TERRIFIC DAY,
Y'ALL!! ♥

## October 5

How people treat you
is their karma...
but how you react is yours!
Respect is a TWO way street!!
Remove ALL the negatives
from your life and
FOCUS on
ONLY the POSITIVES!!!
Hold your head high and
know your karma just keeps
getting BETTER and BETTER!!
After all, KINDNESS IS FREE!!!
Today~ try giving
more than you get!

## October 6

Holding on to hurt
ONLY hurts YOU!
Forgiveness is the beginning
of ALL healing!
Receive God's forgiveness
for yourself and
generously give it away to others!!
Forgiving others is
LOVING yourself!!
When we take the high road
the view is much more beautiful!!
Wishing EVERYONE a
BEAUTIFUL day!! ♥

## October 7

There are three kinds of people:
those who make things happen,
those who watch things happen,
and those who
wonder what happened.
SO COME ON!
It's Monday morning…
start of a NEW WEEK!
New chances! New choices!
New opportunities!
Which kind of person
are YOU going to be today?
Let's ALL go
MAKE IT HAPPEN!!

## October 8

TODAY is short and sweet~
Do something nice for someone
FOR NO REASON
other than KINDNESS!!
Make it a SUPER DAY, Y'all!! ♥

## October 9

Every day, you get a
NEW CHANCE
to be do or be
whatever YOU WANT!! ~
"Just as the white snow falls
and covers all the ground,
so shall your blessings upon us!
…everything has a time
and a season…"
~Ezekiel 34:26
Make TODAY
your time and season!!

## October 10

We are all capable
of making a difference in others!!
It may be
in the words we speak
or a smile we give.
It may be
the hand we reach out
to help with
or the phone call
they never expected!
Your significance will not be
found in the advancement of self,
but in your impact on others!
TODAY… Let your light shine!!

# October 11

We only get
so many opportunities
in this world
and if you make the CHOICE
not to act on them,
someone else will!!
Today…
look at yourself in the mirror
and say
'TODAY is the DAY
that I MAKE MY DREAMS
COME TRUE!!'
Now get on out in the world and
DO IT!!
SHINE ON!!

## October 12

I believe…
Joel Osteen says it BEST~
'Oftentimes, people allow
the opinions of others
to hold them back
and water down their dreams.
But, we have to realize
that there will always be critics
and naysayers in life.
One of the most important things
you can learn is that other people
don't have to believe in you
for your dreams to come to pass.
Other people don't set the limits
for your life… YOU DO!'
Set those limits HIGH today
and FLY!! ♥

# October 13

You should be more concerned
with what you are
than with what you have!!
What you have
won't get you into Heaven,
but what you are will!!
Just remember~
If you will tend to God's business,
he will tend to yours!!
Stay Focused! Stay Faithful!
Stay Encouraged! Stay Strong!
Stay Kind! STAY POSITIVE!!
Now go make it a
THRILLING DAY!! ♥

# October 14

On this Columbus Day,
we should all do a little
soul searching and goal searching
and set a course
for a new adventure!!
Let go of fear,
cast away from the shore
for the unknown and
see where you land!!
What you discover
may surprise even you!!
DREAM BIG! WORK HARD!
DISCOVER NEW WORLDS!!
Happy Columbus Day, Everyone!!
♥

# October 15

HAPPINESS is a CHOICE!
No matter
what is going on
around you,
your attitude
is ALL up to you!!
Start by putting a smile
on your face
then a skip in your step, and
if you really want to feel good~
focus on helping someone else!
Today, I wish everyone a very
HAPPY DAY!!

## October 16

Life is too short to hold grudges.
Find it in your heart to forgive!
And move on with your life!!
You will find so much more joy
when you do!
Forgiveness FREES the soul!
Carrying anything
other than love in your heart
only hurts you!
Today I wish EVERYONE
Peace and Love!

# October 17

We were EACH created to be
AMAZING INDIVIDUALS!!
Each of us
COMPLETELY UNIQUE!
Each a true ONE OF A KIND!
When we compare ourselves
to others, we are denying
our own possibilities!!
Listen… Labels are meant
for soup cans, NOT PEOPLE!
Break out of the mold today
and SHINE!!
Show the world how
BRIGHT of a STAR
you really are!!
BE BRAVE!!
BE DARING!!
BE YOURSELF!!!

## October 18

You DO NOT have to be
a product of your environment!
At some point,
your past is no longer an excuse
for your present
or lack of a future!
Don't feed your fears!!
Feed your purpose, your passion,
your creativity, your inspiration,
your hopes, and your Soul!
When you
LIVE WITH PASSION,
you regret less, appreciate more
and can rise above any past
experience to be AMAZING!!

# October 19

When you focus
on the lives of others,
you aren't working on YOUR life!
Today… refocus on YOUR LIFE
and GET MOTIVATED to
make it the life you want to live!!
Out the door EARLY today
to a modeling job for Neiman's,
then a quick meeting with my
agency and finally FOCUSING on
a new and exciting TV Show
I'm working on!!
HAPPY WONDERFUL DAY,
Y'ALL!!
Grab your coffee
and let's get FOCUSSED!!

## October 20

The TRUE worth of a person
is not in what they own
or how much they make,
but in how much they give
without need
for anything in return!!
Those who give
'expecting' a return
are NOT truly giving!
Today… HELP SOMEONE
not because it's
the right thing to do,
but because you want to,
expecting nothing back!
Then the return can truly be felt!
Wishing EVERYONE a VERY
GIVING and LOVING day! ♥

## October 21

Too often…
people don't realize that
climbing over someone,
attempting to
destroy or harm someone
may get you somewhere
in the short term,
but once the truth
of how you got there
is revealed...
Consequences must be paid!
Your INTEGRITY
will always be remembered
longer than your prosperity!!
Wishing everyone a GRACIOUS
and FABULOUS DAY!!

## October 22

I know that being
REALLY happy
is not having what you want,
it's WANTING
what you've already GOT!!
Life is about appreciation!!
What are you
GRATEFUL for today?
When you live your life
with gratitude,
it turns your attitude
into gladitude!!
SHINE ON!!

# October 23

Knowledge…
is knowing when you can't.
Faith…
is knowing that God can!!
Wisdom…
is finding a solution in chaos!
Courage…
is making a change
even through the fear!
"Just as the white snow falls and
covers all the ground, so shall
your blessings upon us!
…everything has a time
and a season"
~Ezekiel 34:26
Make this week
YOUR Time and Season!!

## October 24

'Train yourself
to live in the present,
without regretting the past
or fearing the future.'
…is a recipe for a happy life!!
Being alive is a gift!
Being happy is a choice!!
Choose to MAKE IT a
HAPPY and POSITIVE day!!
Now grab some coffee and
Let's go make our dreams
come true!!

# October 25

PLEASE don't ever lose
that light inside of you!
You know…
the one that gives you
the power!
The power to
BELIEVE IN YOURSELF
…that you can achieve anything!
The one that allows you
to shine like the
ORIGINAL ART WORK
you are!
Do everything you can
to foster growth in your light and
CRANK UP THE WATTAGE!
We weren't created to be dull!
We were created to SHINE!!!
Hoping EVERYONE SPARKLES
and SHINES today!! ♥

## October 26

It doesn't matter
where LIFE takes YOU…
it matters where YOU take LIFE!!
Don't let the words of others
mold you,
let YOUR actions define
who you REALLY are!!
Being true to yourself and
BEING YOURSELF
are the GREATEST gifts
you can give this world!!
Happy YOU Day!!
Time to CELEBRATE!!
♥

## October 27

Heard an amazing quote
last night and I wanted to share it
with everyone today! ~
'Family is more than just DNA.
It's about people who care and
take care of each other!'
So look around at your 'Family'
…they are the ones
who help you thru life!
They are the ones
who encourage you to
SPARKLE and SHINE!!
Today I want to say
THANK YOU to EVERYONE
who encourages and
helps others thru life!!
KEEP IT UP!! ♥

## October 28

I know that the battle
belongs to the persistent..
the victory will go to
the one who never quits!
Winning doesn't start around you,
it begins inside YOU!
No matter how long
the road has been,
how many struggles
you have faced or
how many times
you have been told it's impossible
~ VICTORY BELONGS
to those who KEEP GOING!!
Now go MAKE IT a
VICTORIOUS DAY!!

## October 29

This Halloween time…
remember to trick yourself into a
POSITIVE HAPPY ATTITUDE
and treat yourself
to tons of FRIENDS and FUN!!
Life is short!
Enjoy every moment!
Love with ALL of your heart!
And help as many people
as you can!!
Happy AMAZING Day,
Everyone!! ♥

## October 30

In Genesis, God created
the whole universe
out of nothing!!
Next time you think
you have nothing, ask God
to make something out of it!
It's NEVER too late
to start something new!
It's NEVER too late
to make your dreams come true!!
Start with prayer,
add a ton of faith and
give it ALL to God!!
Don't forget along the way,
to fill your heart with gratitude!

## October 31

I believe that
for every up there is a down,
for every smile there is a frown,
but for every night there is a day
and for every dream…
there is a way!!!
Don't let go of your dreams!!
Wishing EVERYONE a
HAPPY HALLOWEEN
filled with Spooky Fun and
FANTASTIC TREATS!!! =)))

# November

## November 1

If you BELIEVE
you can do something,
then you will.
The struggle to find
the FAITH in yourself and
the FAITH in God
is what either keeps you from it…
or brings you to it!
So today, I ask~
What do you BELIEVE
you can do?
START BELIEVING MORE
and fearing less!!!

## November 2

Too often, people quit too soon
to avoid the 'storms' of life!
But you must remember,
when your storm is at its worst,
watch for the rainbow!!
God's light will break through
the clouds and surround you
with beauty and radiance!!
You'll never know
how CLOSE you are
to realizing your dream
if you quit!
So stick to the FIGHT and
MAKE YOUR DREAMS
come TRUE!!

## November 3

Today I am quoting the
AMAZING Zig Ziglar,
who I am so EXCITED to be
meeting on Friday night!!
"Your ATTITUDE,
not your aptitude,
will determine your ALTITUDE!"
So get your attitude right and
see how high you SOAR!!
FOCUS today only on
positive thoughts and
stay the course,
focused on the goal!!
Who knows where you will
wake up tomorrow?
See you on top…
with a BIG cup of COFFEE!!
LOL

## November 4

Everyone experiences
tough times…
it is a measure
of your determination
and dedication
as to how you deal with them and
how you can come through them.
Maybe when you think
things are falling apart,
everything is really
falling into place?
Life works in mysterious ways!!
Keep the FAITH and
don't forget to SHINE!!

## November 5

I heard the most
beautiful song last night~
'If I can help just one person
along the way… then my living
will not be in vain!'
So today I ask you~
when was the last time you
HELPED a stranger?
When was the last time you
offered help to a friend?
THIS DAY is a great day
to START making sure
your living is NOT in vain!
Remember, God does not require
us to earn HIS love
and we must not
require others to earn ours!

## November 6

Happiness can only come
once you allow yourself
the possibility and resolve
to open your heart to it!
You must believe in yourself first!
For if love doesn't require
some sort of sacrifice on our part,
we probably aren't
loving the person at all!
Today, be grateful
for the sacrifices
made FOR YOU!!
Wishing everyone today
a HAPPY and LOVING DAY!!
♥

# November 7

As humans, we are driven
by ONLY two forces~
Passion and Fear!
If what we seek
we are passionate enough about,
we WILL MAKE it happen
but if what we fear is stronger,
then success will never be yours!
Let go of fear!
So you fail...
Get back up and TRY AGAIN!
FOCUS on what you want,
CREATE honest passion
for it and then
GO GET IT!!

## November 8

Confidence is admitting
who you are,
what you've done, and
loving yourself for
who you've become,
no matter what others
think of you!
After all, there is never a
guarantee in life…
only opportunities.
When you spend all of your time
worrying and stressing
on your fears,
you miss out on greater things!
So go forth today
with CONFIDENCE
and seek out each opportunity
to be SUCCESSFUL!

## November 9

Reminding everyone this morning
to BE CAREFUL
about what you focus on!!
Every little thought
that creeps in MATTERS!!
And here is why~
When you focus on
what you don't have
or your failures,
it defeats your ability to
TURN THINGS AROUND!!
But when you
focus on POSSIBILITIES,
you will have more
OPPORTUNITIES!!
Today, focus on what 'could be'
and turn it into 'what is'!!

# November 10

After asking everyone
last night at the event,
'What is your favorite attitude
to see on a woman?'
the consistent answer was
CONFIDENCE!!
So today…
I want to remind EVERYONE,
not just women,
that when you know yourself,
you are empowered!
But when you
ACCEPT YOURSELF…
you are invincible!!
Go forward today
with the confidence
that you can be INVINCIBLE!!
And don't forget the coffee!!
LOL =)

# November 11

Courage is letting go
of the familiar
to make a better future.
Never let fear keep you
from moving forward
with your life!!
At times, you must walk away
from the familiar
to fight for a brighter tomorrow!
It's like Winston Churchill said,
"Fear is a reaction.
Courage is a decision."
I wish everyone a very
COURAGEOUS and
FABULOUS day!! ♥

## November 12

When things happen in your life
that don't make sense to you,
and you don't understand why,
it's because God has taken control.
So when you feel lost,
look at your GPS –
God's Placement System,
and though you still
may not know where you are,
TRUST that you will arrive safely
and exactly when and where
you should!!
Wishing everyone
a very FAITH-filled day!!

# November 13

Welcome to a new day
full of hope and possibilities!
Enjoy it FULLY and don't forget~
it doesn't take long to be kind…
help someone if you can!
"I will praise you,
O Lord my God,
with all my heart,
and I will glorify your name
forevermore!"
~Psalms 86:12
Wishing Y'all
a very blessed day!!
♥

## November 14

You should remove the things
in your life today
that are not in line
with your dreams for tomorrow!
Dreams are life's opportunities
waiting for you
to MAKE them real!
I believe dreams
can become reality,
so long as YOU set goals
and keep pushing forward!!
You CAN do whatever
your dreams inspire!
So, what are YOUR goals today
for a SUCCESSFUL tomorrow?
Let's go MAKE our
dreams come true!!
♥

# November 15

I believe that hardships
make us strong!
Problems give birth
to wisdom!
And sorrows
cultivate compassion!
When you are given a struggle
in life to get thru,
look for the lesson!
It's God's way of showing us
WE CAN DO ANYTHING
if we want to!!
All the strength we need
lies within us!!

# November 16

Complaining about a problem
in life doesn't make it go away,
instead, it actually increases
your focus on it
in a negative way!
Stop complaining and
START PRAISING!!
Praise all the things RIGHT
in your life!
Praise the problems from the past
that you have overcome!
When you put your mind
back into POSITIVE MODE,
the solutions become clear!!
Make it a POSITIVE MINDED
and FILLED day, Y'all!!
Now let's begin
WACKY
WONDERFUL DAY!!
=))))

# November 17

Sometimes we just need to hear~
'STAY THE COURSE!'
If it feels like your troubles
come and go~
'STAY THE COURSE!'
If you feel like you aren't sure
what you want out of life~
'STAY THE COURSE!'
If it feels like your dreams
won't come true~
'STAY THE COURSE!!'
Keep FAITH as your guide and
ALL your DREAMS
WILL COME TRUE!!
For when we keep abiding
is when we start rising!!
Praise along the way and
when you reach shore,
SMILE and THANK God for an
AMAZING journey to your
HAPPY destination!! ♥

# November 18

If this week
wasn't all you wanted,
take the weekend
to readjust your plans, and
rest and prepare
for a successful next week!!
Life will ONLY BE
what YOU MAKE IT!!
Don't quit!!
Keep dreaming!!
Keep striving!!
God rewards those
who stay in FAITH!!
Time to start believing in YOU!!
YOU CAN DO IT!!
Now let's all go have a
FABULOUS DAY!!
I'm starting with COFFEE!!
♥

# November 19

I am thanking God today
for ALL of my friends!!
Friends are the family we choose!
They laugh with you,
cry with you,
hold your hand
when you're scared and
ENCOURAGE you
to KEEP GOING!!
Friends are like angels on earth
who protect us from danger, and
give us a little push
when we need it!!
Today I want to say ~
'THANK YOU TO ALL
MY FRIENDS!!'
In my humble opinion...
YOU ROCK!!
♥

# November 20

Everyone should LET GO
of their anger, jealousy,
and hatred for others!
They are ALL negative emotions
and create a hardened heart!
Free yourself from such pettiness!!
RISE ABOVE the desire
to post negative thoughts!
Spread LOVE instead!
Spread GOODWILL!
Spread PEACE!
"Do your best to live with
everyone in peace."
~Romans 12:18
We need to make a new holiday…
HAPPY DAY!!!
No bad news... no bad talk...
nothing bad…
just a day to smile and laugh!!
A BLESSED day to ALL!
♥

# November 21

I would like
to wish everyone
a very
HAPPY THANKSGIVING!!!
When you focus
on all the things in your life
you can and
should be grateful for,
your life begins
to fill with HAPPINESS!!
Today, take the time to say
'THANK YOU' to ALL those
you are grateful to!!
Thank YOU ALL
for being my friend!!
Now go get your
Gobble-Gobble on!! =))))

# November 22

Real happiness
comes not in achieving
big things,
but in enjoying and appreciating
the simple blessings in life.
God has a plan and
A purpose for you,
so don't let negative thoughts
or words hold you back
from your TRUE potential…
you are better than that!!
Remember~
Positive speaking and
positive thinking
results in positive actions!
Who's ready for a
POSITIVE DAY?
♥

# November 23

Watch what you focus on
because THAT is what
you will bring to pass!
If you are always
thinking you can't,
you never will!
Start thinking YOU CAN!
Focus on Solutions…
NOT problems!!
Remember, Fear is what separates
you from your potential!
Success doesn't come to you…
you go to it!!
Now go MAKE IT
a FOCUSED and
SUCCESSFUL Day!!
Time to SHINE!!
♥

## November 24

There are two facts to consider~
firstly… happiness is a choice, and
secondly… no one can choose
your happiness but yourself!!
Happiness is waiting for YOU,
so stop waiting for it!!
Look in the mirror and repeat...
'Today, I'm going to be HAPPY!'
And then keep repeating it
ALL DAY long!!
Now go and have
an INCREDIBLY HAPPY and
MAGICAL DAY!!
♥

# November 25

I believe…
that every trial we face
comes from the hand of God,
who wants us to grow.
If you are wise enough,
you will see that
disruptive moments
are really divine appointments…
preparing you
for the next lesson in life!
With FAITH,
there is nothing to fear!
My grandma always said,
'fear is a lack of faith in God!'
She NEVER worried!!
And God ALWAYS provided!!

# November 26

We should all FOCUS
on what makes us UNIQUE!
When you look at others
with envy or jealousy
you are only
bringing yourself down!
God made you a
ONE OF A KIND!!
An original work of art!!
CELEBRATE your
UNIQUENESS!!
Celebrate YOU today!!
♥

# November 27

The holiday season, to me,
is a time of reflection…
a time to look back
at what has gone right, and
where you veered off the road.
Don't let yourself get down
when you look back, instead,
let it LIGHT A FIRE in you!!
Let it create a PASSION to want
to change things for the better!!
The pitiful person goes nowhere,
but the powerful person
sets their course and
starts planning the climb!!
Passion unattended
is the flame that burns
to its own destruction!
FAN THE FIRE!!
SET THE COURSE!!
Prepare for SUCCESS!!

# November 28

I believe that when
WHAT you WANT
becomes IMPORTANT
enough to you,
you will find a way
to make it HAPPEN!
Until then, it is just a thought,
dream or aspiration.
Don't let life pass you by
while you are not deciding!
Take today and DECIDE on
WHAT YOU WANT!
Then go MAKE IT HAPPEN!

## November 29

I wonder why some people
find it easier to judge
and condemn others, than to
INSPIRE and ENCOURAGE?
Watch the video on my wall and
GET INSPIRED!!
It doesn't matter
what God gave you...
IT'S WHAT YOU DO WITH IT!!
Pretty doesn't come
from how you look…
it comes from how you ACT!!
Go out today and be
BEAUTIFUL!!

# November 30

I believe that…
changing ONE thing for the better
is worth more than
proving a thousand things
that are wrong!!
When you spend your day
focused on the negative,
YOU BECOME THAT!
Focus instead on the POSITIVE!
Rise above pettiness and
learn to SHINE!!
Some people want it to happen,
some wish it would happen,
and others make it happen!!
Which one are YOU
going to be today?
Now let's grab some coffee and go
MAKE IT HAPPEN!!
♥

# December

# December 1

If you struggle in life,
you should know~
you aren't alone!
Everyone struggles everyday
with the small and big things!
Learn to appreciate
small victories.
Where there is no struggle,
there is NO STRENGTH!
YOU are STRONG!!
Remember that
and then be GRATEFUL
for anything and everything!!
Hey, you have to
go THRU something
to HAVE something!!
Now put a smile on your face and
have a Thrilling Day!!
Time to SHINE!!
♥

## December 2

If you want to get over a problem
you must stop thinking about it!
Your mind affects your mouth,
and your mouth affects you mind!
You don't have to have
certain things happen
in order to start feeling better
about your life,
you just need to focus
on the right things!
Let go of the negative, and
feel the love!!
We all need to work on this on!!
Make it a FABULOUSLY
FOCUSED day!!

## December 3

No two people are alike,
except twins, and yet
I think people are
MORE ALIKE than different!
We all want to be accepted
for who we are!
We all want to be loved
and appreciated!
We all have feelings
that can either be lifted
or hurt by others!
So today, when you look
at the people you don't like
or approve of… STOP!
…and look in the mirror!
I bet if you were HONEST,
you would find
a lot of similarities!
The key to understanding people
is understanding that you
are no better than anyone else!

## December 4

Today… I will remind myself to
"Be strong and courageous,
for the Lord your God
is with you wherever you go."
AND "I can do all things through
Christ who strengths me."
~Philippians 4:13

## December 5

When you live in PASSION,
good things happen!
Don't wait for something
exciting to happen to
get passionate ~
GET PASSIONATE and
something exciting WILL happen!
Don't drag thru life!
Do it to the BEST of your ability!
Sow the seed of greatness
that lies within you TODAY!!
Happy Passionate Day, Y'all!!

## December 6

YOUR future begins NOW
by what YOU do!
Make sure to love yourself
enough to generate the fire
and desire to
accomplish your goals!
Dream BIG because
ANYTHING is possible,
if you set your mind to it!
Make plans, believe in yourself,
and go for what you want!
Remember…
dreams are just opportunities
WAITING to become real!!

## December 7

'Tis the season to be thankful
for all you have~
Never take ANY of it for granted!
Keep on loving and
keep on living!
Being Jealous of anyone
or any situation
isn't going to help you
advance in life.
You're only slowing
yourself down by being
Envious and Self-absorbed!
Look BEYOND self
to see how you can
HELP OTHERS and suddenly
life gets much BRIGHTER!!
Take a hold of your
GRATITUDE and GENEROSITY
this Holiday Season and
Don't forget to SHINE by
SHARING!!

# December 8

When you use lies to hurt people,
the only person who ends up
getting hurt is the one who lied!
Being transparent and real
is the more honest approach!
Anyone who takes the time
to purposely try to hurt
another person,
shouldn't be a part of your life!
I don't ever want to understand
that kind of evil!
We ALL deserve HONESTY,
LOVE and COMPASSION!
You know what they say,
'the TRUTH shall set you free!'
My grandmother taught me~
'TREAT OTHERS as YOU would
have them TREAT YOU!'
Today is chance to show others
the LOVE you want in your life!!
Happy THOUGHTFUL Day!!
♥

**December 9**

We don't quite know
where our paths will lead us,
but we should know how
to embark on the journey~
STAND FIRM,
WALK TALL, BE HUMBLE
and LOVE DEEPLY!
Stand firm in your beliefs,
walk with dignity,
remember we are ALL human and
ALL deserve COMPASSION!
Make it a FANTASTIC Day and
don't forget to
LET YOUR LIGHT SHINE!! =))

## December 10

The best people in life
don't have the best of everything...
they are the ones who
make the best
of everything they have!
When we learn to be grateful and
happy for what we have and
where we are in our lives…
that is when God gives us more!
Celebrate what you have and
who you are!
You are a ONE OF A KIND!
Now go SHINE
like ONLY YOU can!!

**December 11**

Decide today
that you won't give up
on your dreams and desires.
Keep pressing forward,
believing that you are
anointed and empowered.
God's Word encourages us
that we can pray for anything,
and if we believe,
that we WILL receive it!!

# December 12

WE ALL
DESERVE SUCCESS!!
WE ALL
DESERVE HAPPINESS!!
WE ALL
DESERVE LOVE!!
If you don't get HAPPY
where you are NOW,
you will never get to
where you WANT to be!
YOU must SOW the SEED of
GREATNESS in YOU…
find the
PASSION and ENTHUSIASM
that lies within you
and GROW IT!
YOU CAN DO IT!!
Today is a GREAT day to
SHINE!!

# December 13

There are four things that can
never be recovered…
the stone after it's thrown,
the word after it's spoken,
the occasion after it's missed,
and the time after it's gone!
Be careful of what you say
for it cannot be removed
from one's memory!
Spend time with those you love,
for once they are gone,
you WILL wish you had more!
TREASURE
each moment of time,
for once it has passed… it is over!
EYES OPEN TODAY
to every little experience and
smile and be GRATEFUL
for them ALL!
A life filled with gratitude has no
room for negative or sorrow!

# December 14

While you can't go back and
make a brand new start,
you can start from now and
make a brand new end!
It's NEVER too late to
MAKE your dreams come true!!
Every success starts with a plan
of action to get there ~
small steps
emanate strong results!!
So get those feet pointed
in the right direction and
START MOVING!!!
It's a great day to SHINE!!

## December 15

Please don't ever lose
that light inside of you!
The one that is UNIQUE
only to YOU!
You know, the one
that gives you the power…
the power to believe in yourself…
that you can achieve anything!
The one gives you the strength to
SHINE BRIGHTLY!!
The one that makes you... YOU!!
Make sure to
SHINE TODAY!!

# December 16

The holidays can be a time
of feeling empty or sad
and comparing our lives
with others
as the year comes to an end,
BUT DON'T!
Far too often, we depend on others
to make us happy, when really
all we have to do is look
in the mirror and realize happiness
starts within ourselves!
Switch your view
from what you don't have
to what you DO have!
BEING GRATEFUL
BRINGS HAPPINESS!!!
So get your attitude of gratitude
adjusted to ON!!!
Now go make it
a FANTASTIC day!!

# December 17

We should rejoice
in everyday miracles…
the smile of a friend,
the warmth of love.
Don't take them for granted
because you never know where
life is going to take you.
Remember, a coincidence
is just God's way
of performing a miracle
anonymously!
Hope EVERYONE'S day
is filled with
MAGICAL MIRACLES!! =))

## December 18

We should not be afraid
to SHINE!
God created each of us
with unique talents and
disregarding those talents
is like disregarding God!
Don't compare your talents
with others~
they are ALL different!
Be BRAVE and
accept YOUR path and
SHINE BRIGHTLY in his name!
"For God did not give us
a spirit of timidity,
but a spirit of power,
of love and of self-discipline."
~2 Timothy 1:7

## December 19

Remaining calm in adversity
is a sign of great spiritual strength.
No matter what's going on
in your life right now,
'Hold your peace!'
Set your mind, that no matter what
is going on in your life,
you will have a good attitude!
A POSITIVE ATTITUDE
will turn any day around!!
Make this Day One of
VICTORY and COMPASSION!!

# December 20

Never let anyone
steal your joy.
Life is too precious
to waste time on negative people!!
Turn hate to love,
change poison to medicine,
and replace doubts with dreams.
Stop complaining if
you don't like how things are!
Take control, decide how YOU
are going to change it,
think positively,
get rid of the drama,
and MOVE FORWARD!
Every day you have been given
is a gift.
No matter what obstacles
you may encounter,
promise yourself to
make the best of it,
and count your blessings
along the way!!

## December 21

I want to remind you today
that you are not a size,
you are not a weight,
you are not a color,
you are not an age,
you are not a trophy,
you are not a doll,
you are a HUMAN, and
you are BEAUTIFUL!!
Never let others define you...
you define yourself!!!
May you always be treated
the way you treat others!
So go out there and
MAKE SOMEONE'S DAY
HAPPY today!!
Trust me,
It works in BOTH directions!!

**December 22**

My wish for everyone today is
PEACE in your world,
LOVE in your hearts,
LAUGHTER in your lives, and
HOPE in your souls!
Being happy doesn't mean
everything is perfect,
it means you've decided
to see beyond the not-so-good
stuff and enjoy every day!!
The choice to be HAPPY is yours!
CHOOSE AGAPE TODAY!!
And don't forget to
SPREAD a little GOOD CHEER
while you are at it!!

# December 23

During the holidays,
it is easy to look at what
others have and
where their lives are
and wish you had some of that,
but DON'T!
Remember, God has called you
to be you, not someone else!!
Don't 'dim' your light
if you were made to SHINE!
In the end, you will know
a tree by the fruit that it bears!!
So get EXCITED about today!
Get out there and
CREATE JOY in others and
HAPPINESS within yourself!

## December 24

For those of you struggling
this holiday season,
I want to remind you
that even though you
may have a problem,
as long as the problem
doesn't have you~
YOU ARE A CONQUEROR!!
Look above it and,
while you are looking UP,
ask for help!
Worry increases pressure,
but PRAYER releases it!!
Stay in FAITH!!
It's Christmas Eve,
MIRACLES ARE ABOUT
TO HAPPEN!!
♥

## December 25

My prayer today
is that the Host of Angels
brings you
Gloriously Good News,
the Wise Men
bring you Wisdom,
and the miracle of Baby Jesus
blesses you abundantly with
Peace, Love and Happiness!
Merry Christmas
to all of you and your families.

## December 26

You can be confident today
that every dream God
has put in your heart
will come to pass
if you believe with all your heart!
Look inside yourself and
start moving towards your goal!
God can't guide you
if you aren't MOVING!!
Don't let the negative thoughts
creep in and disrupt you!
STAY POSITIVE!!
STAY MOVING!!
Don't give up!
Instead, look up!
Now get out there and
MAKE IT a
MOTIVATED DAY!!

## December 27

Most of the time,
your biggest enemy
is the self doubt
YOU inflict
on the situations
YOU face!
Today,
instead of choosing
the negative view~
CHOOSE THE
POSITIVE VIEW!!
Look for that little place
inside you that wants
VICTORY and
START CLAIMING IT!!
Be your own cheerleader and
believe in YOURSELF!!
And when you look around,
you will find others
who believe in you, too!!

## December 28

Life is not always prefect,
but it is ALWAYS
what you make it!
So make it count,
make it memorable and
never let anyone
steal your happiness!
Comfort is never found
in attempting to sidestep
difficult circumstances,
but in bravely facing them
with the strength that
God provides.
Wishing EVERYONE a
WONDERFUL day!
Get out there and
MAKE IT SHINE!!
♥

# December 29

I want to remind you today
not to be a victim
of circumstance;
instead, be a
beneficiary of possibility!
If you look for the positive
in something
you will find it.
If you look for the negative
in something,
that is all you will see!
The world is full of possibilities,
achievable goals, and
unlimited imagination!
Allow yourself to
FOCUS on the POSITIVE!
Look at each opportunity as an
INCREDIBLE POSSIBILITY!!

# December 30

Have YOU set your
New Years Resolutions?
I have a few I'm working on!
LOL~
The truth is, in life we NEED to
set goals and make plans!!
They are what keep up going…
keep us TRYING!!
As long as you are trying,
you are WINNING!!
Remember, God doesn't
choose the qualified,
God qualifies the chosen!!
Now get out there and
SHINE your way into 2013!!
♥

# December 31

When you treat people
as they are,
they will remain
as they are,
but when you treat them
as they could be,
they can become
what they should be!!
See others
thru eyes of compassion,
not eyes of
judgment or jealousy!
Treat everyone around you as
YOU would have THEM
treat you!
Wishing everyone a
Supercalifragilistic day!!!
Time to SHINE!!!
♥

Made in the USA
Lexington, KY
16 August 2019